F-86 SABRES
OF THE 4th FIGHTER
INTERCEPTOR WING

OSPREY AVIATION

OSPREY FRONTLINE COLOUR

6

F-86 SABRES
OF THE 4th FIGHTER
INTERCEPTOR WING

Warren Thompson

First published in 2002 by Osprey Publishing
Elms Court, Chapel Way, Botley, Oxford, OX2 9LP

ISBN 1 84176 287 3

Edited by Tony Holmes
Page design by Mark Holt
Cutaway Drawing by Mike Badrocke

Origination by The Electronic Page Company, Cwmbran, UK
Printed in Hong Kong through Bookbuilders

02 03 04 05 06   10 9 8 7 6 5 4 3 2 1

EDITOR'S NOTE

To make the *Osprey Frontline Colour* series as authoritative as
possible, the editor would be interested in hearing from any
individual who may have relevant information relating to the
aircraft/units/pilots featured in this, or any other volume
published by Osprey. Similarly, comments on the editorial
content of this book would also be most welcome. Please
write to Tony Holmes at 10 Prospect Road, Sevenoaks, Kent
TN13 3UA, Great Britain, or via e-mail at:
tony.holmes@osprey-jets.freeserve.co.uk

For a catalogue of all books published by Osprey
Military and Aviation please write to:

**Osprey Direct, PO Box 140, Wellingborough,
Northants NN8 2FA, UK
Email: info@ospreydirect.co.uk**

**Osprey Direct USA, c/o MBI Publishing,
729 Prospect Ave, PO Box 1, Osceola, WI 54020, USA
E-mail: info@ospreydirectusa.com**

Visit Osprey at **www.ospreypublishing.com**

FRONT COVER *A flight of 335th FIS F-86Fs display their polished
aluminium finish and the bold Indian head squadron badge
painted on the fuselage (Eusebio Arriaga)*

BACK COVER *The third jet ace of the war, Capt Ralph 'Hoot'
Gibson poses by his Sabre just after a mission. Gibson was
assigned to the 335th FIS and finished his tour with five
confirmed kills. He and the second ace, Capt Richard S Becker of
the 334th FIS, scored their fifth victories on the same day –
9 September 1951. Years after the war, Gibson would fly with the
USAF's aerobatic team,* The Thunderbirds *(A J Walter)*

TITLE PAGE *Lt Drury Callahan is suited up and ready to do battle
with the MiGs. Note that his helmet displays the 334th FIS
badge, and that the squadron colour was red. During autumn
1952 MiG activity increased to the extent that September saw
the second highest tally of MiG kills with 64. This was exceeded
only in June 1953 when 78 were achieved (Drury Callahan)*

TITLE VERSO PAGE *Maj James Jabara pulls in after his final
mission at the completion of his second combat tour in Korea.
Jabara became the first jet ace in May 1951, and his final tally
was 15 confirmed kills, ranking him behind only top scorer Capt
Joseph McConnell (Larry Hendel)*

CONTENTS

LEFT *With external fuel tanks full and guns loaded, this mixed flight of 334th and 335th Sabres prepares for a combat air patrol over 'MiG Alley' from Kimpo in January 1953. The F-86 squadrons scored an above-average 39 confirmed kills during this month due to increased MiG activity (Drury Callahan)*

INTRODUCTION

8 November 1950. The Korean War is entering its fourth month, and high above the rugged terrain near the Yalu River that marks the boundary between North Korea and Manchuria, an element of US fighters is providing top cover for some fighter-bombers. Lt Russell J Brown is flying one of the fighters (an F-80C Shooting Star called *Ilene M*) when six silver swept-wing jets jump the USAF formation out of the sun. As they dive past, the American pilots react aggressively.

Five of the newcomers head back over the river, but Brown has locked onto the sixth. His wingmen hear him say over the radio 'damn, I'm going to get him'. As the other aircraft bottoms out of its dive and its speed slackens, Brown fires several short 0.50-cal bursts at it. Almost immediately fire breaks out in the stricken aircraft's fuselage and it explodes.

The first battle between jet fighters is over in a matter of seconds. Air combat has just entered a new era.

BACKGROUND TO WAR

In the late 1940s the Cold War was gathering momentum. The western alliance and the eastern bloc communist countries confronted each other in Europe, but the clash between them would come far away, in one of the more remote areas of the Far East – the Korean peninsula.

The conflict followed the Soviet Union's late entry into the Pacific theatre of World War 2, and the US offer to share with it the task of ending the Japanese occupation of Korea. The peninsula was divided at the 38th parallel of latitude, and in 1948 Kim Il-Sung was installed as leader of the northern territory, styled the Democratic People's Republic of Korea.

Although the US had backed the south, a series of ambiguous statements from Washington alarmed the government in Seoul about the true nature of American intentions. For example, in January 1950, in a speech to the National Press Club in Washington, Secretary of State Dean Acheson appeared to omit the Republic of Korea from the area the US was committed to defend. Kim Il-Sung, fanatically determined to place himself at the head of a unified nation, interpreted this as an invitation to invade South Korea.

And although Washington had been kept informed of the massive build up of Soviet-supplied military equipment in North Korea, the warnings had been virtually ignored. The result was not long delayed.

THE NORTH INVADES

In the early hours of 25 June 1950, under cover of bad weather, North Korean tanks rumbled over the 38th parallel to begin the invasion of the south. There was little to stop them. South Korean forces were no match for Kim's army, and US reinforcements were too little and too late. The United Nations (UN) called on North Korea to abandon the invasion, and authorised the use of force against it.

But in late June 1950 it seemed nothing could stop the North Korean army from investing the whole peninsula.

By August UN-backed forces were defending a shrinking perimeter around the port of Pusan in south-east Korea, their backs to the sea. The situation was desperate. To relieve it, UN commander-in-chief Gen Douglas MacArthur ordered an invasion of northern-held territory, and on 15 September US Marines waded ashore at Inchon, near Seoul. Soon, Kim's armies were retreating, and by 20 October the North Korean capital Pyongyang had fallen. It really did look as though MacArthur would make good his boast of 'bringing the boys home by Christmas'.

But just over a month later China entered the war. Thousands of troops swarmed across the Yalu and plunged UN forces into headlong retreat. After weeks of bitter fighting the line was stabilised, and apart from an unsuccessful Chinese onslaught in April 1951, the ground war remained virtually static for the remainder of the conflict. Talks aimed at achieving a cease-fire would drag on at Panmunjon until the conflict finally ended in July 1953.

WAR IN THE AIR

In the air UN forces held the initiative virtually from the start. Although the North Korean People's Air Force (NKPAF) had been greatly expanded with Soviet-supplied aircraft, they were mostly of World War 2 vintage, and no match for the US Far East Air Force (FEAF). Based in Japan, it was equipped with numerous types including F-80 Shooting Stars, F-82 Twin Mustangs, B-26 Invaders and, at Guam, B-29 Superfortresses. The NKPAF was crushed within two weeks, its flyable remnants being forced to seek safety in Manchuria. For the next four months UN aircraft were able to roam over North Korea virtually unhindered. This all came to an end on the first day of November 1950.

That afternoon, south of the Yalu, F-51 Mustangs from the 18th Fighter Bomber Group (FBG) sighted two swept-wing jet fighters of a type not seen before. Over the next three days the sightings increased, and the F-80's days as the fastest fighter in Korean skies were numbered.

It was just a matter of time before the F-80 met the mysterious new fighter in combat, and Lt Brown's victory made headlines the world over. It certainly made an impact in Washington, for three days later orders were cut sending the 4th Fighter Interceptor Wing (FIW) to Korea. The USAF was committing its latest fighter, the North American F-86A Sabre, to take on the mysterious swept-wing Soviet-built jet, which the world would soon know as the MiG-15.

The battleground for this new style of air combat would be limited to a small portion of north-west Korea, bordered by the Yalu River and the Yellow Sea. Pilots would call it 'MiG Alley'.

Warren E Thompson
Germantown, Tennessee
March 2002

CHAPTER ONE

THE SABRE'S COMBAT DEBUT

BELOW *Two squadrons of F-86As (334th and 335th FIS) were crammed on the deck of USS* Cape Esperance *at San Diego and shipped to Japan in November 1950 in rapid response to the MiG-15's sudden appearance over North Korea (John Henderson)*

When the situation is critical, the United States military can process paperwork with lightning speed. With the safety of friendly ground forces and air superiority over Korea at stake, orders were issued on 11 November 1950 for the 4th FIW to leave immediately for Korea. Just hours later 49 Sabres were taking off from three different bases on the US east coast on the first stage of the flight to Naval Air Station North Island, San Diego, that took them via Wright-Patterson, Kirtland and Williams AFBs.

Aircraft of the wing's 334th and 335th Fighter Interceptor Squadrons were embarked on the escort carrier USS *Cape Esperance* (CVE-88) for Japan. The remaining Sabres of the 336th FIS were flown to

McClelland AFB and taken by barge to Oakland, where they were to travel as deck cargo on a fast tanker. The carrier took 13 days to reach Kisarasu, Japan, and once the damage caused to the F-86s by salt spray corrosion during the voyage was repaired, the aircraft were flown to Johnson Air Base (AB), near Tokyo.

4th FIW/4th FIG

The 4th FIW was one of the USAF's top combat units. Designated the 4th Fighter Group during World War 2, it had been credited with the destruction of more than 1000 German aircraft in the air and on the ground. In 1950, the squadrons comprising the 4th were the 334th

LEFT *Lt Col Glenn Eagleston was an eyewitness to the MiG-15's devastating firepower six months into the 4th FIW's tour in Korea. It did not take too many hits from the slow-firing 37 mm N-37 cannon to inflict heavy damage, or even to blow a Sabre's wing off. Eagleston flew his F-86 safely back to Johnson AB, Japan, where it was declared fit only for the salvaging of spare parts (John Henderson)*

ABOVE *336th FIS CO Lt Col Bruce Hinton poses by an F-86A several months after claiming the 4th FIW's first MiG-15 kill. Sabre pilots had to fight knowing that they would be running low on fuel when the air battles began. Many were forced to glide back to base in South Korea completely out of fuel (Malcolm Norton)*

'Pigeons' (later the 'Eagles'), 335th 'Chiefs' and 336th 'Rocketeers'. The first component to reach Korea was a combat group headed by the wing's Commanding Officer, Col George F Smith, which arrived at Kimpo AB, also called K-14, near Seoul in December 1950.

In 1950, like all USAF combat wings, the 4th FIW assumed the identity of the World War 2 group of the same designation, but continued to control a subordinate combat group until 1952. Between 1952 and 1993 the USAF dispensed with combat groups, which meant that frontline squadrons reported directly to wing headquarters.

INTO COMBAT

Records state that the 4th FIW's initial temporary duty to the Far East saw a total of 131 officers and 413 enlisted men make the move. These figures included pilots and support personnel. The responsibility placed on them was considerable, for they were about to enter an uncertain arena in which the enemy's capabilities were relatively unknown. Indeed, as they settled into their temporary bases in Japan, the question on every pilot's mind was just how tough would the new MiG be, and what were its characteristics, especially its strengths and weakness?

Intelligence sources were of little help. All they had to go on were camera-gun pictures and sketchy descriptions provided by F-51 and F-80 pilots who had usually viewed the aircraft from afar. One thing was known for certain though. The MiG-15 could climb faster than anything seen before – an ominous portent of its capabilities, especially when flown by an experienced pilot. And another thing – the MiGs would be flying just a short distance from their Manchurian bases, leaving them with plenty of fuel for a fight. The F-86s, on the other hand, would have travelled about 200 miles by the time they arrived in 'MiG Alley'. They would be low on fuel, for even when fitted with two 120-gallon external drop tanks, the Sabre's combat radius was only about 500 miles.

On 15 December the 4th FIG CO, World War 2 ace Col John C Meyer, led a detachment of F-86As from Johnson to Kimpo. Group records state that at 1550 hrs on the same day, seven Sabres flown by pilots of Detachment 'A' and the 336th FIS left Kimpo for the North Korea-Manchurian border. Although this flight was performed primarily for orientation and familiarisation purposes, it represented the Sabre's first venture over enemy-held territory. It was uneventful, as no MiGs were sighted, and another mission scheduled for the following

day was cancelled due to bad weather. The first clash was postponed, but not for long.

FIRST KILL

On 17 December 336th FIS CO Lt Col Bruce N Hinton led a flight of F-86s on a combat air patrol along the Yalu River. It did not take long for them to arouse some attention, and the flight's No 2 man warned of four bogies flying in a south-easterly direction toward the Sabres. The No 3 pilot called that they were swept-wing jets. Hinton describes that historic first encounter;

'We were headed 040 degrees at 25,000 ft. The MiGs were flying at approximately 18,000 ft. We immediately proceeded to turn into them, diving all the way. The bogies were already in battle formation, and went into a climbing right trail. We continued our turn, pulling about 5G, and distinctly out-turning the MiGs. They seemed to lose integrity as they observed us coming in. They levelled out on a heading parallel to the Yalu River.

'We continued to close in, with our airspeed at about 410 knots at 20,000 ft. At that moment the MiGs dropped their external fuel tanks, with thick white foam coming from the falling tanks. For an instant, they dived and then abruptly began climbing left to turn. Our

airspeed at this time was above red-line. The enemy pilots began spreading out, with their No 4 man breaking left and with friendly Nos 3 and 4 chasing MiG Nos 1 and 2. I gave the one in front of me a short burst, which scored multiple hits on his right wing, causing fuel to leak out.

'My armour-piercing incendiary rounds impacted all over the MiG's fuselage. At this point he appeared to be in trouble. While in a gentle turn to the left, he popped his speed brakes for about two seconds, then pulled them back in. I manoeuvred out of his jet wash and positioned myself about 800 to 1000 ft behind. In a perfect firing position, I fired a long burst that went up his tail pipe. Seconds later, fire began coming out of the rear of the MiG, along with heavy smoke that momentarily obstructed him from view.

'As the enemy fighter began to decelerate rapidly, I pulled up so as not to collide with him. Moving into position again, I fired another long burst that caused the smoke to be replaced with a huge plume of flames, which enveloped the entire MiG. Another burst of 0.50-cal rounds caused pieces to come off the fuselage and wings. It suddenly did a reverse turn and got on its back, slowing down and losing altitude rapidly in a steep dive. The smoke trail went straight toward the ground

ABOVE *Lt Ward Hitt of the 336th FIS taxies out for another fighter sweep through 'MiG Alley'. Note the symbols painted on the side of the Sabre which indicate his mission tally. By the end of December 1950 the 4th had claimed eight confirmed MiG-15 kills and two probables for the loss of only one Sabre (Ward Hitt)*

approximately ten miles south-east of the Yalu, below 10,000 ft. No explosion was seen.'

All told, Hinton fired 1500 rounds to bag his MiG.

While he was scoring the F-86's first confirmed kill, two of the 336th FIS Sabres had engaged the other element of MiGs. They zeroed in on the No 4 jet, and pushing their airspeed to 0.98 Mach, were slowly gaining. Then the communist pilot made a left turn and headed straight down toward the Yalu, accelerating rapidly. This MiG had been fired at from a long distance, forcing its pilot to leave the area. One of the Sabre pilots reported seeing an aircraft pouring smoke and fire, heading straight for the ground – Hinton's MiG.

The first major confrontation had ended in favour of the F-86, but the battle between the two jets was just beginning. The 4th FIW's pilots now knew something else about their opponent – when the MiG dropped its nose and accelerated, it was extremely fast. Indeed, in this first engagement two machines had used their speed to escape unscathed.

Five days later, on the morning of 22 December, the stage was set for a much larger duel. Two F-86 flights were cruising at 35,000 ft when they encountered several MiGs, and the ensuing dogfight was brief but intense.

It would also be the first time that the Americans experienced the effect of the opposition's heavy calibre guns. Capt Bach was caught from behind as he broke hard right, 37 mm rounds hitting his wing root and causing his F-86A (49-1176) to begin a series of violent snap-rolls. Bach punched out and became a Prisoner of War (PoW). This was the conflict's first Sabre loss.

But Bach's capture was soon avenged that afternoon in what would prove to be one of the F-86's most successful fights, considering the odds. Only eight jets participated in this combat air patrol, but once the dust had settled their pilots had scored six confirmed MiG kills.

The flight leaders on this occasion were two of the most experienced pilots in the business – Col John C Meyer and Lt Col Glenn T Eagleston, both of whom were high-scoring Mustang aces from World War 2. At the climax of the battle there were elements of MiG-15s scattered from 32,000 ft down to tree-top level. As fuel was running low, some of the F-86s started working their way back to the south. One element spotted two MiGs at 9000 ft and could not pass up the opportunity this offered. Within a minute both enemy jets had been shot down. The victorious Sabres were led by Eagleston, with

BELOW Before the 4th FIG finally settled in at Kimpo, its squadrons were scattered around South Korean bases such as Suwon and Taegu. When the Chinese pushed UN forces past the 38th parallel, the group was briefly forced back to Japan in late 1950. Taegu-based Sabre 49-1297 was lost on 13 July 1952 (Tex Badger)

LEFT *Capt James Jabara (far left, with cigar) mingles with other 4th FIG pilots outside the briefing tent. This picture was taken in May 1951 before Jabara had knocked down his fifth and sixth MiGs to become the USAF's first jet ace of the Korean War. Although assigned to the 334th FIS, he was flying a mission with the 335th FIS when he 'made ace' (Ed Fletcher)*

Lt John Odiorne as his wingman. Meyer had one of the more spectacular kills that afternoon when, flying at 20,000 ft, he got in a high-deflection burst at a fast-moving MiG. His rounds impacted all over the aircraft, causing it to disintegrate.

Several facts emerged from the subsequent debriefing. First, the importance of the 'two-ship' element, even in fast-moving high-Mach fights, was clear. It also seemed that most MiG pilots tried to set up their firing positions from the rear, but in each case the Sabre wingmen were able to keep their 'shooters' informed, enabling the F-86s to emerge without loss. Kills were credited to Meyer, Eagleston and Cdr Paul Pugh (USN), all from 4th FIG HQ, Capt James Roberts (335th) and Lts Arthur O'Connor (336th) and Odiorne (334th).

On the final day of December, the 4th sent 33 Sabres to patrol the Yalu around the town of Sinuiju. These were split into two different flights which were staggered in timing so that as the first ran low on fuel the second came on station. The weather was perfect but the MiGs stayed on the ground. This trend continued into 1951.

Group records state that in the final two weeks of December 1950, 234 sorties had been logged, and MiGs had been engaged 76 times. The results were eight officially credited kills and two probables for the loss of one F-86.

Detachment 'A's' existence at Kimpo ended on the afternoon of 2 January 1951, when the Chinese advance threatened UN bases in the northern sectors of South Korea. All tactical aircraft units, and personnel, were evacuated to Itazuke and Johnson ABs in Japan, the 4th going to the latter site. Enemy forces were very close to over-running Kimpo when the last USAF units pulled out, with the two 51st FIW F-80 squadrons being among the last to leave. Indeed, the enemy was so close by then that pilots reported dropping their ordnance on communist forces just two minutes after departing Kimpo!

TEETHING TROUBLES

The loss of their Korean base put the F-86 squadrons in a difficult situation, for they were still required to fly through 'MiG Alley' on a daily basis, but the added distance placed a heavy strain on both pilots and maintenance crews. And that was not all. According to records kept by North American technical representative John L Henderson, who accompanied the 4th to Korea, there were some minor problems to be solved once the Sabre went into action. One of the more serious concerned canopy visibility. Henderson recalls;

'After the first combat mission, the pilots complained of poor to no visibility through the back half of the transparent canopy bubble because of icing. The forward part was kept clear by direct air across the inside from

OPPOSITE In early 1951 Sabres were using Suwon and Taegu as forward bases. Conditions at both sites were poor compared to those in Japan, which is why this 334th Sabre is undergoing an engine change out in the open. Such open-air maintenance became particularly problematical in the winter months (Ed Fletcher)

perforated tubes alongside the canopy tracks. There was no direct air application for defrosting onto the canopy behind the pilot. In other words, it was impossible for the pilot to check his "six o'clock" position either in the rear view mirror or by looking back over his shoulder. Two remedial actions were taken. One was to add a length of tubing to the existing auxiliary system and extend it further back in the cockpit to get some airflow to the rear. This improved the situation somewhat, but not enough to get into a full field modification.

'The greatest improvement came when the inside of the canopy was cleaned by the maintenance people before a mission. This was a time-consuming job, but it paid off. This meticulous routine continued for the duration of the Korean War.'

In fact, even before leaving the US the F-86As had to undergo some minor modifications which saw their nose gear strengthened and elevators 'beefed up' to withstand high-G manoeuvring.

Conserving fuel was a priority for the Sabre pilots, for fuel consumption could not be allowed to interfere with the mission, especially as combat air patrols had to maintain high airspeed to counter sudden attacks. North American's John L Henderson again;

'It has been written that many Sabre pilots flew single 120-gallon drop tank patrol missions over North Korea – more than one pilot returned to base with one drop tank still installed and empty. But an F-86 take off with an asymmetrical loading of over 800 lbs under one wing was never documented as a mission profile! I have been unable to confirm that single tank missions were flown in test or in combat.'

The consumption rate of these drop tanks was phenomenal. They were also very expensive, but without them the F-86 would have been limited in range, leaving the fighter-bombers unprotected as they struck targets along the Manchurian border. The need to maintain F-86 patrols kept the pilots logging additional cockpit hours as a result of these long flights, but two weeks later, on 17 January 1951, combat operations returned to Korea when the 335th FIS sent its Sabres to Taegu AB (K-2).

Records show that between 17-31 January, the number of aircraft available for operations by the squadron varied from four to eight. Pilots were rotated

LEFT *Lt Orren H Ohlinger of the 334th FIS prepares to fly another long mission up to the north-west corner of Korea in February 1951. At this time the 4th FIW was operating from Johnson AB due to the Chinese threat to South Korean bases. Ohlinger was credited with a MiG-15 kill on 16 October 1951 (Al Beaty)*

frequently so that as many as possible could gain valuable combat experience against the MiG-15s. From Taegu, the squadron flew several types of mission – armed reconnaissance, close support under 'Mosquito' control (forward air controllers in AT-6 Texans) and combat air patrols. The 4th FIW's official history states that some missions were flown with a full 0.50-cal load only, or with full ammunition, two 5-inch High-Velocity Aerial Rockets under the wings and maximum fuel, which included the external tanks.

And when the B-29s started to conduct hazardous daylight missions, the F-86s became embroiled in some of their most complex and vicious fights with the MiGs. Usually, Sabre top cover was co-ordinated not only with the bomber stream, but also with the slower fighter-bombers that were attacking targets close by. With the F-86 screen having to provide protection for both strikes

simultaneously, these combat air patrols proved difficult to plan, with the fighters' timing on station being of critical importance. Often, the Sabres arrived slightly early or late, and sometimes the B-29s were not on time. But they could always rely on the MiGs being airborne, ready to oppose the big Boeing bombers.

B-29 TOP COVER

One of the first bomber escort missions was flown on 8 July 1951. F-86 pilot Maj Frank L Fisher participated in the sortie;

'There were 32 Sabres from the 334th and 336th squadrons which were to rendezvous with a dozen B-29s. The bomber stream was making its bomb runs in three-ship boxes. A swarm of F-51s from the 18th FBW was assigned the job of flak suppression 30 minutes prior to the bombers' time-over-target. Sixteen of us were

BELOW By the spring of 1951 more communist jets were appearing over 'MiG Alley', yet the 4th FIG was still the only F-86 outfit committed to combat. The Pentagon was, however, making plans to convert a Korea-based F-80 group to the new F-86E as jets became available from the North American assembly line (Al Beaty)

ABOVE *In late January 1951 MiG-15s with bright red noses began appearing in large numbers, and Sabre pilots reported that their attacks were well-executed, with aggressive follow-through. Due to this improvement in the competition, it was decided that all future CAP missions should comprise at least 16 Sabres. This 334th FIS F-86 (50-687) flew numerous such missions over North Korea during the early days, and was eventually lost on 2 July 1952 whilst still on the strength of the same squadron (George Ola)*

Two new aircraft types arrived in Korea in December 1950, namely the F-84 and the F-86. Shown at Taegu the following spring are 4th FIG F-86s and a solitary 27th FBW F-84 Thunderjet. The latter would take over the fighter-bomber role in the largest numbers after UN forces had stabilised the frontline to ensure the safety of South Korean bases (Guy Brown)

ABOVE *The threat of night attacks from NKPAF Po-2 biplanes was real, and for a short period F-86s parked at Suwon AB were covered in camouflage netting to conceal them from the intruders. There was no real answer to these nuisance attacks because nightfighters had trouble matching their speed to that of the slow Po-2s (James Leatherbee)*

placed directly over the bombers at 0.86 Mach, performing "S" turns at 25,000 ft. The remaining 16 set up a screen ahead of the formation, and to its north. The Mustangs did their job well and the bombers were over their target on time.

'Coming off the bomb run, the formation turned left about 150 degrees to head south-east back to their base at Okinawa. Some of our F-86s shifted back to make sure the last of the bombers were well protected. All was quiet and the sky was clear. With our fuel starting to run low, we were thinking about a gentle descent into our base at Suwon (K-13). Suddenly, a lone RF-80 pilot who had come in behind the bombers to take pictures called on our channel. He said he was at high altitude over "MiG Alley", and that a large number of MiGs had just passed under him headed south in the direction of Pyongyang. My fuel was low, but enough to get back and check it out. "Diamond lead, this is Elgin, can we break escort?" Bomber lead immediately released us, and I told all F-86 flights to head for Pyongyang if fuel permitted.

'My flight came in at 25,000 ft heading west, with the sun high and a little south. In minutes we had them – a large gaggle of about 40 MiGs just beginning to roll over into a dive. They were going after our F-51 flak suppression

group, who were cruising back home in formation far below at about 5000 ft. They were sitting ducks. The MiG commander had probably held his aircraft down while he monitored our progress, figuring we would be low on fuel. At that time he launched his group to clean up the Mustangs, expecting no interference from us.

'The MiG leader was already in his dive, with the others right behind, when he caught sight of my flight rolling in behind them. Without hesitation, he pulled out of the dive to meet us head-on as we came down. His intake scoop was aimed straight at me. As he flashed by, I could see his helmet and shoulders. It was more like an impression than a conscious glance. The nose of his MiG was red, along with parts of his fuselage and tail, against gleaming silver. Suddenly there were MiGs everywhere.

Seconds later I noticed that some were diving away and heading north while the remainder were pressing the dogfight. You could tell they were all startled by our appearance. They were also about 100 miles from their base at Antung. This was the furthest south we had ever fought them, and it felt like we were finally fighting over our own turf.

'What was set up to be an easy score had turned into a hornet's nest of activity, with the enemy worried about

fuel consumption and disengagement tactics for the first time. Fortunately for them, all the F-86s were extremely low on fuel, and this limited our fight and pursuit toward the Yalu. Had we caught them with our internal tanks full, it would have been a big day for the 4th. I closed on a MiG diving at about 5000 ft, ranging with the throttle grip to about 3000 ft – a bit too far out yet. Suddenly, the MiG rolled left and pulled up level some 2000 ft away, with me sitting in his ''six o'clock''. I gradually closed to 1500 ft, and my first burst hit his rear fuselage a little too high. A few pieces of the MiG flew by me as I lowered the pipper by two feet and fired another burst.

'At that second, I caught a shadow off to my right and stopped firing. It turned out to be a pair of F-86s coming down fast through the space between the MiG and my aircraft. They were in a bank, cutting me from their view. We were about to collide. I did a quick right roll and then got back on track, looking for the MiG. I spotted him down low at about 500 ft. As I jockeyed into position again, the MiG hit the top of a hill and a huge orange and black fireball erupted. His engine came flying up in my direction as I hurtled by the explosion. Looking back over my shoulder, I saw large chunks of the MiG rotating as it went down the side of the incline.

'At the debriefing that evening we discovered we'd lost no Sabres in the action, and four MiG-15s were reported destroyed and several damaged. It seems that the reconnaissance pilot who warned us about the MiGs

BELOW *Lt James W Leatherbee's Sabre has been fitted with the 120-gallon drop tanks which were standard equipment for CAPs over North Korea. Sabres engaged MiGs on 76 out of a total of 234 combat sorties in December 1950. This meant that over 150 tanks were dropped in the first two weeks of F-86 combat missions, and this high consumption rate was maintained through to 1953 (James Leatherbee)*

MAIN PICTURE *Lt James Dennison's A-model Sabre (49-1218) sits ready for its next mission at its temporary base at Suwon in the early spring of 1951. At this time several new MiG-15 regiments were rotating into Manchurian bases for training against the F-86s. This Sabre would survive the war to be shipped back to the US for service with a unit operating from Long Beach, California, in 1954 (James Dennison)*

INSET *When the Chinese pushed F-86 operations out of Korea, Sabres were forced to operate from bases in Japan such as Itazuke, where this photograph was taken by an F-80 pilot in February 1951. On 6 March the 334th FIS began staging out of Suwon, and the F-86s would remain on Korean soil until war's end (Ed Fletcher)*

ABOVE *The threat of the MiG-15 gaining air superiority over Korea was always on Supreme UN Commander Gen Douglas MacArthur's mind, for it would have left his ground troops open to air attack. He made this visit to Suwon in March 1951 when the Japan-based 4th FIG was operating one of its Sabre squadrons from the base. At this time the number of MiG sightings reported by fighter-bombers was increasing at an alarming rate (Al Beaty)*

RIGHT *4th FIG pilot Lt Lloyd Thompson poses in the cockpit of Capt Ralph 'Hoot' Gibson's Sabre before departing on a mission. As there were more personnel than aircraft, some junior pilots would have to fly whichever Sabre was serviceable. The red stars painted on the side celebrated Gibson's five kills, and his status as the war's third jet ace (Lloyd Thompson)*

had headed back south after taking his bomb damage photos. He passed right over the fight while we were in the middle of it, and he'd observed a smoking MiG-15 attempting to land at the big airfield at Pyongyang. He reported it had touched down long, went off the runway and began to cartwheel to its total destruction, with a large explosion erupting about half a mile off the runway. This had been a very memorable day for both sides. We were able to save the F-51 Mustang pilots, and that was very satisfying to us.'

But not every pilot was in the thick of the action. Indeed, many men from both the 4th and 51st FIWs only saw MiGs very occasionally. Capt Robert J 'Andy' Andrews of the 335th FIS was one of them;

'On arriving in Japan we set up shop at Johnson AB. It was already crowded before we got there. The 4th also had alert detachments strung out at several air bases in Japan like Misawa and Komaki, in addition to the one at Johnson. At this time, we were flying some combat missions out of Taegu. Finally, in early 1951, when the Chinese were pushed back to the 38th parallel, we started operating out of Suwon, which was a mass of pierced steel planking. At first there was room for only

one squadron, then two and finally we were able to accommodate all three, along with some support units from our main base in Japan.

'I saw MiGs on only a few occasions. On one mission, someone called for a break as we were jumped by MiGs from our "nine o'clock" above 33,000 ft. I rammed the stick hard to the left while simultaneously pulling it into my gut. Away she went into a series of violent snap-rolls. As you can imagine that ended up with me spinning from 33,000 ft downward. I fought it all the way down to 5000 ft and prepared to pull the handles. I let go of the stick and it must have felt sorry for me because it came out of the spin all by itself. I was quite a bit north of the Yalu River as I completed my low-level "acrobatic" flight over Manchuria.

'I had spun the F-86 before back at Langley AFB when I was No 4 in a combat spread formation. In that incident, I pulled it out at tree top-level. From that day over the Yalu, after performing my "acrobatics", I picked up the nickname of "Acro Andy", which I still have today. Soon after that, I became "D Flight" commander in the 335th FIS, and the sign over our tent read "Acro Andy's Array of Attractive Aggressive Aviators".'

BELOW When this photograph was taken at K-14, only one wall of the 4th FIG's mess hall was painted with colourful scenes, cartoons and emblems. By war's end all four would be decorated with murals (Ray Prozinski)

CHAPTER TWO

THE MIG-SABRE BATTLES HEAT UP

BELOW *Each of the 4th FIG's three squadrons kept strict records of its kills, probables and damaged claims. They were posted on scoreboards outside squadron operations – here is the 334th FIS's board at Suwon in April 1951. Capt James Jabara has four kills, and on 20 May he would get his fifth (and sixth) to become the USAF's first jet ace (Al Beaty)*

By early 1951, RF-80 tactical reconnaissance missions along the Yalu were revealing an almost daily increase in the number of MiGs parked on the Manchurian air bases of Antung and Mukden, yet they were not coming south of the river in greater numbers. UN Intelligence theorised that the units operating these machines were just biding their time for a an all-out assault, or that these bases were key training grounds for MiG operations. Either way, these machines posed a potential problem for the FEAF, and the 4th FIG in particular.

At this stage of the war, the number of Sabres in-theatre was just keeping pace with the attrition rate.

This meant that if a large force of MiGs attacked the fighter-bombers, the F-86s providing top cover would be hard-pressed to handle the threat. On 6 March, the 334th FIS began staging patrols out of Suwon, despite the base boasting just a single concrete runway surrounded by a quagmire of mud. By the end of March the entire squadron was flying routine maximum-strength patrols, but encountering no increased enemy fighter activity.

Despite the Sabres' presence, dealing with the B-29s and fighter-bombers was still regarded by the MiG units' as their top priority because of the damage being inflicted on high-value assets along the river. As a result, the bombers found themselves becoming more vulnerable to concentrated MiG attacks during January and February 1951, and daylight missions were soon considered too dangerous for piston-engined medium and heavy bombers such as the B-26 and B-29.

Lt Richard F Merian was flying F-86s as this time, and he had moved with the unit to Suwon from Japan. Here, he recalls the increasing MiG activity south of the river, and also his experiences as a wingman;

'I had several missions under my belt before I ever saw my first MiG. I was participating in a group-strength mission, with two squadrons strung out at different altitudes. A very large battle developed into what looked like a swarm of bees, with everyone trying to line up on everyone else. The leader of my flight was a guy from wing HQ. I hadn't flown with him before. He just kind of cruised through the whole fight without firing his guns. It was an interesting experience flying No 4 in a flight of four. I knew what to expect when flying as a wingman for many of the experienced guys in my squadron, but when your leader came down from wing HQ, you didn't know much about them.

'Fortunately, I was able to fly wing for some of the great ones – Meyer, Billy Hovde, Eagleston and Gabreski to name a few. I remember one time I was flying wing for Col Eagleston and we were by ourselves. Before I knew it, we had ten MiG-15s cornered between us and home. We fought our way out, but not before the colonel had relaxed me by radioing, "if you're scared, then so am I".

'When I first shot at a MiG it was way out of range by at least a mile. I remember how surprised I was when I put the pipper on him, pulled the trigger for about four

LEFT *Capt Jabara (left) celebrates becoming the first USAF ace in Korea after claiming his fifth and sixth MiG kills. Jabara was also successful during his second tour, and ended the war with 15 victories. He flew with the 334th FIS on both tours (Leo Fournier)*

seconds and he didn't light up with hits or go down in flames. On the other hand, there were times when I was so close to them that I could see the pilot's black leather helmet, and see where the Russian red star had been removed from the side of the aircraft.

'The MiG had a bad tendency towards accelerated overshoot. At high speed and high G forces the aft end of the swept wing bent up, causing the centre of lift to move forward and tuck the aeroplane into the turn or snap roll it. On more than one occasion I saw a MiG snapping into a spin, whether deliberate or not, I don't know. Our F-86s had the same trait, but not as exaggerated. In a high speed 6G turn, you had to hold forward pressure to keep from snap rolling.

'Our intelligence kept us informed when it looked like new enemy air regiments had been training up in Mukden and were moving down to Antung to engage us. Sure enough, where you'd been fighting guys with red circles around the nose of the fighters, a new group would have red lightning flashes painted on theirs.'

Now there seemed to be multiple MiG units operating in-theatre. On 12 April a bomber formation from Okinawa was assigned to attack major targets in the Sinuiju area, their main objective being a railway bridge. Thirty-nine B-29s were escorted by F-84s at and below their altitude, with F-86s high above in the top cover position. As the bombers began their run on the bridge, all hell broke loose when at least 70 MiG-15s swarmed in from the north. The Sabres had their hands full because they were heavily outnumbered, this being the enemy's first concentrated effort against the bombers. It proved to be a costly learning experience for the communist pilots, who lost ten of their number within minutes.

Once the MiGs penetrated the F-86 cover they ran into a wall of lead from the B-29 gunners. This was probably the first time these pilots had attacked a big bomber formation, and they paid the price, for six of the confirmed MiG losses were from the B-29s' 0.50-cal turrets. Another four jets went down under the guns of 4th FIG pilots. Once again, it was a mixture of 334th and 336th FIS pilots who drew the assignment, and there were some familiar names on the list – Meyer, Hinton, Capt Howard Lane and the future first jet-ace, Capt James Jabara. In this engagement, Jabara scored his third kill, and he was now just a month away from the coveted fifth.

THE FIRST JET ACE

On 1 May the 334th FIS was relieved at Suwon by the 335th. This was a normal rotation to rest a unit making daily patrols over North Korea. On 20 May an unusually large fight was brewing over 'MiG Alley'. Patrols were scattered when friendly radar picked up 50 MiG-15s

crossing the river, and a call went out for all 36 Sabres in the area to converge on the enemy from all directions. The fight was on. Jabara attempted to drop his external tanks when the sighting was called but one hung up, putting him at a distinct disadvantage. Rather than obey the unwritten rule and leave the area with his wingman, he chose to attack. When the brief fight ended, three MiG-15s were destroyed, Jabara claiming two of them for his fifth and sixth kills. He had just become the first American jet ace.

The resulting news media coverage caught the imagination of the public back in the US. The glamour days of the fighter pilot were back, and the duels between the jets in North Korean skies filled the front pages. But this also meant that the work of other combat pilots – no matter how valuable a contribution they were making to the war effort – was ignored. Unfortunately, the media also ignored the high-scoring Sabre pilot's most valuable asset – his wingman. In a flight of four aircraft, they would be the two pilots with the least combat experience, yet their responsibility was considerable. They had to protect their leaders at any cost.

LEFT *Kimpo was one of the war's biggest UN bases, accommodating a variety of aircraft types. After the frontline had stabilised, it served as home for the 4th FIW (F-86s) and the 67th Tactical Reconnaissance Wing (RF-51s, RF-80s, RF-86s and RB-26s), as well as the Royal Australian Air Force's No 77 Sqn (Meteor F 8s) (Richard Erratt)*

One such wingman was Lt Robert W Smith. As a second lieutenant, he did time in F-86As back in the US before his combat tour. He had the privilege of flying wing for Capt Ralph 'Hoot' Gibson when he got his fifth kill to become the war's third jet ace. At the time, Smith was still assigned to the 336th FIS, but was flying in a 335th gaggle;

'I remember watching "Hoot" down that MiG-15, and I was probably mesmerised by the sight. His rounds were hitting the MiG, and they made sparkles like some sort of a pin-ball machine. I thought I was doing a good job keeping his "six o'clock" clear when suddenly I saw tell-tale balls of fire from a MiG's 37 mm cannon passing over my wing. There were four enemy fighters right behind me.

'I immediately called out for "Hoot" to break, but he was too engrossed to be interrupted. His only reply was "can you handle it?" I told him I was going to break off, and immediately broke into the fire. Fortunately, the MiG pilots weren't sharpshooters, and their cannon had a very slow rate of fire. It didn't last as long as it seemed, but those four MiGs made me work from 20,000 ft all the way down to the deck to shake them.

'During some of the violent manoeuvring, I warped my wings to the point that they had to be replaced. I don't know why all four of them came after me and left Gibson alone, but it didn't take long for my fear to turn into rage. At one point, when I had one of them in my sights, I burned out the barrels because the rounds were tumbling ineffectively toward the MiG I was firing at.

'We were far north, close to the river, and I was very low on fuel, but at least I had kept Capt Gibson's tail clear during the fight. I had to shut the engine down and glide

EMERGENCY ESCAPE INSTRUCTIONS
1. LEAN FORWARD & PULL UP RIGHT HANDGRIP TO EJECT CANOPY.
WARNING:—LOWER HEAD AS FAR AS POSSIBLE.
2. PULL UP LEFT HANDGRIP.
3. HOOK HEELS IN FOOTRESTS & BRACE ARMS ON ARMRESTS.
4. SIT ERECT WITH HEAD AGAINST HEADREST. 5. SQUEEZE TRIGGER.

RADAR TARGET IND.

The pilot's view of the A-1CM gunsight mounted in a 4th FIG F-86E. The first 530 A-models off the assembly line had the Mark 18 sight fitted, with the more complex A-1CM only being installed in the final 24 F-86As built, and on all F-86Es. Although the Sabre had radar for automatic ranging, its complexity made maintenance difficult in the field (Ernie Atkinson)

home from 45,000 ft. When I was close enough to enter the pattern, I restarted and landed without incident long after the others. They'd already written me off, so they were glad to see me. What a day it had been. I'd landed with less than ten gallons of fuel in my internal tanks.'

TRAINING – THE KEY TO SUCCESS

At the close of operations on 31 May, the 4th released some figures to the media. The most impressive was that in the first five months of 1951, the group had logged 3550 sorties over North Korea, with 22 MiG-15s confirmed as destroyed in the air without the loss a single F-86 in combat. This was a testament to the pilots' training, and also to the level of experience that new pilots were able to acquire on each flight. Here was the key to the kill ratio which was to be highly publicised at the end of the war.

Many years later it was learned that the Soviets had replaced experienced units with air regiments lacking combat time. This supports the F-86 pilots' speculation about the arrival of new training classes, whose pilots initially lacked aggression. But their quality changed radically during June and July, and it quickly became obvious that the

inexperienced units had been replaced by squadrons manned by seasoned combat pilots – possibly veterans from World War 2. It was speculated that they were from East Germany, Czechoslovakia, Hungary or other Warsaw Pact countries.

USAF intelligence reckoned that not only were these better pilots ('honchos'), but that they were also bringing their own aircraft with them. This could explain the periodic change in markings. Another popular theory was that the MiGs were being flown on a regular basis by North Korean, Chinese and Soviet pilots. It was suggested that the North Koreans generally flew at between 15,000 and 25,000 ft, with the Chinese at the intermediate altitudes of 25,000 to 35,000 ft and the Russians at the highest levels. Of course, many of these theories were exploded in the mid-1990s when the Russians became more open about their activities during the Korean War.

THE E-MODEL ARRIVES

Both the Pentagon and the North American engineers were well aware of the F-86A's short-comings, and many improvements were consequently incorporated into newer models. The next off the line was the F-86E, examples of which began leaving the North American facility on 9 February 1951. Construction of the E-model had been completed by May.

By the late summer of 1951, Fifth Air Force believed that over 450 MiG-15s were based in Manchuria. Yet the 4th FIW had only 89 Sabres available in-theatre (Japan and Korea), of which just 44 were committed at any one time from Korean bases. This produced a rather lop-sided margin in favour of the MiGs, but the F-86As would have to hang on until the autumn.

When faced with such overwhelming odds, even the more experienced pilots suffered an occasional bad day, particularly when they discovered the destructive power of a 37 mm shell. Glenn Eagleston, now 4th FIG CO, was on the receiving end of some accurate cannon fire from a MiG-15 on 28 June 1951. In a vicious dogfight, one of the enemy fighters hit his Sabre in the middle of its port gun compartment, whilst several more 23 mm rounds impacted further back on the fuselage. The aircraft lurched out of control from 30,000 ft down to 15,000 ft, but Eagleston fought it all the way and finally levelled off and headed south. Considering the damage, the fighter's engine ran only slightly roughly, but there was enough control for the ace to make a safe landing at Suwon.

Once parked, the damaged jet was examined by the groundcrews and a curious group of pilots. They saw that underneath the three 23 mm holes was three feet of collapsed air intake duct, heavy damage to the engine accessory cover and two turbine blades, along with gaping holes in the tail cone and dorsal fin. One of the port-side machine guns had also been completely blown out. If this was a warning about the MiG's destructive power, it was also a testimony to the F-86's ruggedness. But the MiG's guns were slow-firing, and this gave the Sabre pilots time to break – providing the first couple of rounds missed.

MiG pilots also had the ability to zoom back up to high altitude after a high speed diving pass. Maj Philip Van Sickle, 335th FIS CO, recalls;

'Our mission was to fly top cover for fighter-bombers. My four-ship flight was climbing through 35,000 ft, and our aircraft each had two external fuel tanks. One of the pilots suddenly called out a bandit at "six o'clock high". I saw him diving down on us from the rear, and called out for the flight to jettison tanks. I made a turn to the right and then rolled over and headed down to pick up some badly-needed airspeed. This manoeuvre could best be described as an offside loop. When we came up on the

front side of the loop, I spotted the MiG pulling straight up to his altitude perch, where I expected him to stay. On the first pass he overshot us and went underneath our flight.

'On reaching altitude the MiG pilot immediately rolled over and came down at us again from the rear. This surprised me, as normally they would make their first firing pass and zoom back up to altitude, where they stayed until another F-86 flight passed underneath. After this first loop my four-ship flight was still intact, but then one of the pilots in my second element called out that two more MiGs were trying to get in on the act. Since I had my hands full, I told the element to take them. By this time, my wingman and I had picked up enough airspeed to fight effectively.

'Our target was still in our "six o'clock", but out of effective range. We were now manoeuvring in a true vertical loop. Jockeying for the advantage continued for five consecutive loops, with my wingman and I gradually gaining position on the MiG with each one of them. At the bottom of the fifth loop we had worked our way into the MiG's "six o'clock", and were rapidly closing to effective gun range.

'Suddenly the MiG pilot pushed forward on his control stick, causing me to lose sight of him beneath the nose of my Sabre. I followed suit, placing negative-G on my aircraft, which threw me up hard against my straps as I attempted to follow. After losing sight of him for a few seconds, I picked him up again as he pulled back hard and entered his sixth loop. We were right on his tail and in firing range. As he went over the top, he made a rapid roll and started down on the back side of his sixth and final loop. I fired a short burst during his roll but I don't think I hit him. I sensed the MiG pilot realised he'd blown it by hanging in there for as long as he did, and that he should have stayed on his perch. We would never have been able to touch him. Now it was too late, and he knew it.

'My wingman and I were right on his tail going down what turned out to be the final loop. At the bottom, the MiG pulled into a high-G turn to the right. We were about 1000 ft behind when I opened up. I observed strikes from wingtip to wingtip, with many passing through the cockpit area, and this apparently killed him. I was so intent on following the stricken MiG that I didn't realise we were rolling towards the vertical. My wingman yelled at me to roll out. I snapped my F-86 upright and then

RIGHT *F-86E-1s stand alert at Kimpo. With their pilots waiting at readiness nearby, they could be airborne in just a matter of minutes. Note the 335th FIS badge on each Sabre, and the pilots' helmets resting on the windscreen tops. None of the UN airbases was subject to daylight attacks, just night raids by Po-2s (Karl Dittmer)*

ABOVE *Maj Felix Asla Jr (pilot standing to attention second from right) has just been awarded the DFC and Silver Star for his outstanding leadership and skill on F-86 combat missions by 4th FIW CO, Col Harrison Thyng (back to the camera). Asla was killed when his Sabre was shot down by a MiG-15 on 1 August 1952 (Gordon Beem)*

INSET *Helped by his crew chief, the 335th FIS's Maj William K Thomas dons his flight gear whilst standing on the wing of his F-86E-10* Virginia Belle *at Kimpo. Thomas scored a confirmed kill on 31 May 1952, and by the time this photograph was taken several weeks later, the Sabre had been credited with two more victories. Records show that 51-2722 was lost on 4 September 1952 (William K Thomas)*

MAIN PICTURE *A close-up view of* Virginia Belle's *nose. Note that Maj Thomas is listed on the crew stencil painted on the fuselage. This photograph was taken before the 335th FIS badge was applied to the jet's side, together with kill markings for the aircraft's three victories. In March 1952, the 4th lost three F-86s in combat while claiming 39 MiG-15s destroyed – a phenomenal 13:1 kill ratio (William K Thomas)*

watched the MiG crash, inverted, into a mountain several thousand feet below. Glancing at my instrument panel, I noticed we were below 15,000 ft – our fight had begun at 35,000 ft. According to my Sabre's accelerometer, we had pulled 7.5G on some of the manoeuvres. Needless to say, we both we were wrung out after that fight!'

MiG PILOTS' NEW TACTICS

Now the clashes between the MiGs were happening almost daily, and the communist pilots were developing new tactics to counter the F-86s as they protected the fighter-bombers. Pilots had names for each of them. They were known as 'hit-and-run', 'zoom-and-sun', 'yo-yo', 'pincer-and-envelopment', the 'end run', the 'decoy' and the 'uppercut', among many others.

'Pincer-and-envelopment' seemed to be at its most effective when the F-86s were low on fuel. This tactic required the MiG formations to spread out to the east and west and then go south as far as they could without

being detected. They would then converge on the middle of the peninsula, hoping to catch the fighter-bombers or F-86s heading home without enough fuel to fight. This sometimes worked, but with the spaced flow of Sabres heading north, there was usually a fresh flight of them to engage the MiGs. Then the roles were reversed because the Sabres were fresh and the MiGs short of fuel.

The 'yo-yo' tactic seemed to have come into its own in the late spring of 1951. It required a large number of MiGs to orbit in a Lufbery circle about 5000-6000 ft above the Sabre formations. One aircraft would dive down for a firing pass and then zoom back up to the others. This usually happened when 20 or more MiGs were involved, and it kept the F-86 pilots on the defensive, with little or no chance of taking on the entire formation. If the MiG pilots had been sharpshooters, the Sabres would have been in a lot of trouble. The most effective way to handle this tactic was to start diving as the single MiG came down through the formation. When

RIGHT *Three 334th FIS pilots pose by a Sabre on the K-14 flightline. They are, from left to right, Lts Harry Ramsay, John Lowery and Edwin Scarff. In late spring 1952 the 4th FIW used a number of its aircraft as fighter-bombers, and on a few missions carried 1000-lb bombs (John Lowery)*

he bottomed out and started his climb, the pursuing Sabre would have enough airspeed to 'hose' the MiG down with gunfire.

Experienced MiG leaders tried to evolve other tactics to take advantage of the F-86 pilots' aggressive flying. They used decoys in several ways, and in a few cases the ploy worked well, but usually it did not. The tops of some MiGs were also painted in a camouflage scheme to make them hard to spot from above, and this variation of the basic decoy tactic was known among the 4th pilots as the 'stair-case'. It involved about eight MiGs in elements of two, each of which was stepped down and back with at least 2000 ft between them. The lead pair would be far out in front, and they would usually be in polished silver finish, which was easy to see. When the F-86s dived on the front pair, the trailing element would use their superior climbing speed to move in behind. But it was common knowledge that the MiGs did not operate in pairs without a large number of others close by. In this case, experience saved lives.

Lt Gene F Rogge remembers a harrowing mission when the MiGs came in on his flight from behind, and he emerged from the subsequent fight with a kill. Both he and his wingman also experienced several close calls;

'I was the No 3 member (element lead) of an F-86E flight from the 334th FIS on a mission flown in August 1952. The flight was led by a staff member on that day.

We were just south of the Yalu, with my element on the left in a tactical formation at 40,000 ft, when I spotted a flight of four MiG-15s about a mile above us. They were at our "ten o'clock", flying in the opposite direction. I called them out, but flight lead didn't have them in sight, so he continued down the river. They spotted us and started a descending turn in behind us. The leader still didn't have them, so he said to continue. I immediately told him they were almost in firing range, and that we needed to break left.

'He continued to fly straight ahead, and I hesitated to leave the leader as I didn't know what his intentions were. But I did know that if we continued, all of us would be sitting ducks. When the MiGs reached firing range, I called for a hard left break. The lead element continued on down the river, and my element had a fight on its hands. No 4 was at a disadvantage as I broke into him.

'I was initially glad that the bandits had taken us on rather than the lead element because I didn't like their chances. However, as the fight progressed I saw the MiG leader on my wingman, way out ahead and below me. I realised that I had to quit my fight and try to catch my wing. I attempted to call turns to him to help me catch up, but he'd taken a couple of hits and switched to his emergency frequency. He didn't respond, and I needed to close the gap. I was heading down at a transonic speed as they were coming up.

ABOVE *334th FIS pilot Capt Maynard E Stogdill was credited with a MiG kill while flying his assigned F-86, named Gweny. This squadron produced two of the war's top three aces, namely Capt Manuel Fernandez (14.5 victories) and Maj James Jabara (15). Kimpo was the 4th FIG's home base for most of the war (Maynard Stogdill)*

'I pulled some heavy G trying to get a quick cut-off. I fired off a couple of bursts out of range hoping I could distract the MiG – no luck! I then closed into lethal range and put the tracers all over his canopy. The jet burst into flames, rolled over and flew right into the ground. I couldn't avoid going through the fire and debris, but my Sabre didn't seem to suffer any ill effects from the experience. I broke hard, expecting to see three MiGs on my tail, but they weren't there. Next, I called for my wingman but couldn't raise him. I immediately headed south since we had a strict policy of no singles in the combat zone.

'When I landed back at Kimpo, I saw my wing's shot-up Sabre sitting on the edge of the taxyway, abandoned. It was a relief to find out he was okay, and a lot more battle-wise. The gun camera film of my kill was excellent,

and it made many newsreels and film specials. It showed the MiG taking hits and my F-86 flying through the fire and smoke trail, with just the MiG's wingtips showing.'

THE WINGMAN'S VITAL ROLE

The high-scoring Sabre pilots had at least three things going for them in a dogfight – a great fighter, good eyes and a wingman they could rely on. There were many wingmen who finished their tours with no kills or probables, but without their support in a fight, many of the aces would not have survived. Lt Garold 'Ray' Beck, a 336th FIS pilot, remembers the time he flew wing for his CO, Maj Richard Creighton, who was already an ace;

'He had five confirmed kills and had never been shot at by a MiG. On this mission, we were patrolling north of

where the fighter-bombers were working the main supply routes. We were manoeuvring beneath about a dozen MiG-15s some 15,000 ft above us. Suddenly, Maj Creighton said "Keep it in, Red 2" and he started a diving hard turn to the right. I dove and turned with him, pulling 6G and trying to look back to see what was going on to cause the concern, but to no avail because the G was too great, and it was pulling my oxygen mask away from my face.

'My mouth felt like it was full of cotton, and I was breathing as if I'd been running around the circle we were flying. At about 8000 ft, Red 1 rolled out of the turn and levelled off. As he did, I was about 1500 ft to the left of him, and there was a MiG directly behind. I told him to break right, but he didn't. Later I learned his microphone cord was caught on the stick, and he had to get it free before he could manoeuvre. I was committed to the break, and as I did, I saw two MiGs behind me, which followed me part way through a diving, hard right 360-degree turn that took me to the tree-tops at close to 600 mph. When Creighton arrived back at base, he shook his head and told the others he doubted I'd make it back. When he last saw me there were two MiGs on my tail and things were looking bad. But I did elude my pursuers and make it back to base.'

Although relatively few Sabres were lost in combat, there were scores of pilots who found themselves in a similar situation to Lt Beck. They attribute their survival to their training, and also to North American's ability to build a tough aircraft.

These F-86F-10s are heading north with external tanks full. From 1 to 8 August 1952, Sabre pilots claimed 17 MiG-15s destroyed for the loss of only one F-86. This was one of the highest-scoring periods of the war. Shortly after this, the 4th received 200-gallon drop tanks, which increased combat radius by 463 miles (Karl Dittmer)

ABOVE One of the more colourful Sabres of the war, WHAM BAM was assigned to Lt Martin Bambrick of the 335th FIS, whose crew chief is shown here. Flying a combat air patrol on 4 September 1952, Bambrick received credit for shooting down a MiG-15. The 4th finished phasing out its old F-86As in favour of the new E-models in July of that year (Karl Dittmer)

OPPOSITE Experienced 334th FIS fighter 'jocks' Lts Drury Callahan (left) and Horace Mitchell pose on the edge of the Kimpo flightline in May 1952 (Drury Callahan)

THE SABRE'S OTHER VICTIMS

The communist inventory in Manchuria was known to include a significant number of Tupolev Tu-2 twin-engined bombers. They posed a real threat to the frontline troops, but the constant F-86 patrols seemed to deter their use. Even so, at least nine Tu-2 kills were attributed to F-86 pilots, and most of these were downed on one mission on 30 November 1951 when 31 Sabres encountered 12 of the bombers, escorted by 16 La-9s and 18 MiG-15s. One of the pilots involved in the interception was Lt Raymond O Barton of the 334th FIS;

'My second kill of the war wasn't a MiG but a Tu-2 bomber, equipped with "stingers" in the tail – two 20 mm cannon, I believe. We heard they were coming, and encountered them heading south right off the coast of North Korea. I set up for the classic training solution of a turn reversing gunnery curve, but quickly dumped the idea. Instead, I broke left and came back around. This time, I stuck my nose right up the bomber's tail, squeezed off a long burst and it blew up.

'I flew right through the debris, and from the size of the explosion, I think his bombs blew. I broke left again and was going to make another pass when I checked my "seven o'clock" to clear for my wingman. All of a sudden

the SOB started shooting at me and then I realised it was a MiG and not my wingman! It was at this time that I discovered I'd attracted far more than one MiG. I turned into them and kind of bluffed my way out of the first gaggle and tried to call my wingman, but got no answer. So I turned back north to see if I could spot a 'chute or a raft or something, but no joy.

'Now the MiGs were all around me, and I developed a technique of trying to run them out of ammo! I called for help, and the only response I got was from my room-mate, Maj George Davis. I'll never forget his reply. "I don't have enough fuel left either but I'm on the way". All the MiGs except one had left the area. I had a huge hole where my left fuel cap had been, but I was still flying. When George reached me he asked me to make a couple of identifying turn reversals. I reluctantly did, and he shot that SOB right off my butt. We made it home, where I found out my wingman had made it back okay. He'd gone after one of the Tu-2s and we got separated. He latched on to another F-86 for the flight back to Kimpo. My jet was repaired with a new fuel bladder and a filler cap. Amazingly, there was no structural damage.'

Maj Davis was credited with three Tu-2s and one MiG-15 on that mission.

ITCHY FINGER was the Sabre assigned to Lt John S Brandt of the 336th FIS, and it was photographed at Kimpo shortly before the squadron badge was painted on the sides of the aircraft. The 336th ended the war with 116.5 confirmed aerial kills (Jeff Dibrell)

MAIN PICTURE *Spread out at high altitude, this flight of 336th FIS F-86Es converges on 'MiG Alley', with external drop tanks in position. The jets are flying just below contrail height so as to avoid giving away their position, and number. When MiG formations came south, they were usually flying at 45,000 ft or above, which meant that produced tell-tale contrails. So although the Sabre pilots could not climb to their level, they were at least aware of their presence (USAF)*

INSET *With flight gear and 'Mae West' donned, Capt Troy C Cope is ready for action in a high-time Sabre marked with many kill symbols credited to several different pilots. The 'Mae West' was essential because if an aircraft was too badly damaged to reach a friendly base, pilots would have to ditch or bail out over Chodo Island. Either way, they would have to swim for it. Capt Cope was killed on 16 September 1952 flying an F-86F-1 (Robert Jones)*

RIGHT MENDE'S MENACE *was an F-86E assigned to the 334th FIS at Kimpo in 1952. It was rumoured to have been flown by Capt Jabara when he scored one of his kills, but this has not been confirmed. During this period of the Korean War, the group's biggest problem was not the threat posed by MiGs, but flagging morale amongst its pilots. This situation arose because there were so many pilots rotating in from advanced training in the US that it was taking much longer to finish the number of missions required to complete a tour of duty. This problem persisted for quite awhile (C H Diercks)*

BELOW RIGHT *This aircraft was one of the more colourful Sabres to fly with the 336th FIS. The sharksmouth was a rare adornment on F-86s in Korea, although by the end of the war an entire flight of the 51st FIW's 25th FIS at Suwon had adopted this as its symbol. This F-86A-5 was assigned to Lt Joseph Fields. It survived the war and later served with the 123rd FIS at Portland International Airport, in Oregon (Robert Fahey)*

ABOVE *A typical daily scene at Kimpo. Immediately after a fighter-bomber or B-29 strike, one or more photo-reconnaissance aircraft would take pictures of the bomb damage to determine if the target had been destroyed, or if another mission was required. This RF-80A is taxiing out for such a mission, with F-86s forming up to escort it. Usually, the slower RF-80s took off a few minutes ahead due to the speed difference. Note the No 77 Sqn Meteor F 8 taxiing past in the opposite direction* (William Schrimsher)

LEFT *This sign, positioned alongside the flightline at K-14, says it all. Once the pilots finished briefing for the mission, they would walk out under the sign and head to their waiting jets parked on the ramp. The Sabre in the background was assigned to the 336th FIS* (Kenneth Haugen)

INSET LEFT *When it came to engaging communist MiGs, it would be very difficult to better the American fighter pilot. And when it came to horsing around on the ground, these same men also proved hard to beat. These 335th FIS pilots have finished their briefing and are ready to fly the mission, but not before they strike a collective pose for the camera in relaxed fashion (John Myrick)*

MAIN PICTURE
A mixed flight of 334th FIS F-86Es and Fs taxy out for a combat mission against the MiGs in the late summer of 1952. The F-models were just beginning to appears in the group's inventory when this photograph was taken (Jimmie Pierce)

INSET RIGHT *The business end of a gleaming 336th FIS F-86. Pilots complained that the fighter's six 0.50-cal M-3 Colt-Brownings did not have sufficient 'knock-down' power, and that many MiGs took numerous hits, yet still returned to their bases in Manchuria. These complaints resulted in combat testing of the 20 mm cannon in the 'Gun-Val' project of early 1953 (Gordon Edwards)*

CHAPTER THREE

THE FOURTH'S KILL RATIO IMPROVES

The number of enemy fighters coming south of the Yalu was sporadic. One month there would be dogfights involving 50 or 60 MiGs at a time, and the next there would be days between sightings. The reasons for this have never been explained, although there was plenty of speculation from intelligence sources. In June 1952, for example, only 21 MiGs were shot down at a cost of four Sabres – a five-to-one ratio. On the other hand, in the first week of August 1952 17 enemy fighters were destroyed with the loss of just one Sabre.

To the FEAF planners, the Manchurian bases represented a major training centre for oriental pilots instructed by Soviet 'honchos'. The route from Kimpo to 'MiG Alley' lay over the North Korean capital of Pyongyang. Many flights attracted random bursts of flak, which were ineffective, but nevertheless reminded the high-flying Americans of the danger waiting at lower altitudes in this area.

Two seasoned veterans to see action at this time were Maj William K Thomas and Lt Col Francis Vetort,

who had served together in the 56th FIG at Selfridge AFB before the war. On one sweep Thomas flew as Vetort's wingman, and he recalls;

'We discussed tactics if we met up with the MiGs. We took off and settled into a loose finger formation as we climbed. At the bomb line, we test-fired our guns and began a scan of the sky. Pyongyang greeted us with a few bursts of flak. On reaching the mouth of the Yalu, we turned right towards the Suiho Reservoir. Black 3 (Vetort) called and said he had bandits low and to our left. I couldn't see them, so I told him to take over the bounce. Later I discovered that Vetort was carrying binoculars – a habit I adopted too.

'We started down, as Black 3 said he would take the left element and I would take the element leader on the right. I saw four MiGs but later found out there were six! As I closed on my target from a slight angle off to the right, I got a lock-on with the gunsight. At about maximum range I hit the MiG, and he made a violent turn to the right. I could see fire in the aft fuselage, and tried

RIGHT *The 4th FIW's facilities at Kimpo were well endowed with paintings, murals and memorabilia pertaining to the daily visits to 'MiG Alley'. This example adorned the wall of the mess hall in 1952 (Ray Prozinski)*

to get into position for another shot, but was pulling too much G for an effective hit. The MiG was just about engulfed in fire.

'At this time, we were getting a lot of low level bursts, so I decided to climb out of the area. Black 3 called for my position, and said he needed help. We turned back to give him support, but two minutes later he stated that he was all clear and headed south. On the flight back to Kimpo, Lt Col Vetort said he'd shot down a MiG too. We called radar, got a heading to our let-down point and landed without incident. The gun camera film confirmed both our kills.

'After my tour in Korea, I was assigned to the Proving Ground Command at Eglin AFB, where I ran the Fighter Maintenance Squadron. The MiG-15 which had been flown to Kimpo by a defecting pilot in September 1953 was in my squadron, so I became well acquainted with it. I discovered the reason the MiG I shot down had burned so readily was the saddle fuel tanks around the engine.'

IMPRESSIVE STATISTICS

From July to December 1952, the 4th FIG continued to put up as many F-86s as possible for combat patrols.

Maximum effort was required virtually every day, even though the number of MiGs encountered varied considerably. Group records show that the 334th FIS flew 3094 sorties during this period, during which they fired 258,540 rounds of 0.50-cal ammunition. The 335th FIS flew 3234 sorties and claimed 45 MiG-15 destroyed in the air, as well as a further 51 probably destroyed or damaged. Squadron statistics reveal that the unit lost five Sabres in combat, with six others returning safely with battle damage – a nine-to-one kill ratio.

The 336th FIS flew 3408 combat sorties during the same period and claimed 25 MiGs destroyed, with a further 25 probably destroyed or damaged. Kill figures for the 334th FIS were not available for this period. These impressive figures reflect the dedication and skill of the groundcrews who kept so many Sabres flying against an overwhelming number of MiG-15s.

One of the most experienced and gifted Korean War Sabre pilots was 334th FIS CO Maj George A Davis Jr. On his 59th mission on 10 February 1952, he was shot down by a MiG-15 while on a combat air patrol over 'MiG Alley'. He had already destroyed two enemy aircraft during this mission, making him the leading in-theatre ace

ABOVE *F-86E-5 (50-0660) in 334th FIS markings waits on the alert pad at Kimpo for the signal to scramble in June 1952. Each squadron provided an equal share of aircraft and pilots for this assignment. This particular jet was lost in an accident on 28 November 1952 (Drury Callahan)*

ABOVE *F-86A 49-1240 flew with both the 334th and 336th FISs, and survived its combat tour to end up serving with the 190th FIS in the US post-war. It was amongst the last A-model Sabres in Korea when this photograph was taken in June 1952, and its combat career with the 4th FIW came to an end the following month (Drury Callahan)*

with 14 kills at the time of his death. Had he lived, Davis might well have been the war's top scoring ace. On four missions he claimed double kills, and he shot down three Tu-2 bombers in a single sortie off the North Korean coast. Lt William W Littlefield was flying wing for Maj Davis on that fateful mission;

'Maj Davis and I broke away from the rest of the patrol just north of Sinanju. We headed straight for the Yalu to attack MiGs reported to be heading south across the river. About ten miles from the mouth of the Yalu, but still over North Korea, we spotted a gaggle of about ten MiG-15s coming into the "alley". They were about 800 ft below us, and Maj Davis called for a diving turn that would bring us behind them. As we closed in, he started firing at the MiG at the rear of the formation. I saw the enemy's wing root light up from the major's 0.50-cal hits. Billowing smoke immediately poured out of the stricken fighter and it went into an uncontrolled dive towards the ground.

'Maj Davis called out to make sure I was still with him, and we continued right through the formation. He quickly lined up another MiG near the front. His fire impacted all over its right wing root, and like the first one, it started smoking and went straight down in a dive. By this time we had worked our way through the entire formation and were out in front of the remaining MiGs. We were in a very hazardous position, but Maj Davis slowed down to take on the closest MiG. Evidently, one of their pilots had a clean shot at him, and he took at least one or two 37 mm cannon hits. His jet went out of control and crashed into a mountain about 30 miles south of the Yalu River.'

Records show that Maj Davis was flying F-86E-10 51-2752 at the time. He was later awarded a posthumous Medal of Honor. In an unusual move, the Chinese broadcast the name of the pilot reported to have shot him down. He was named as 'the famous air hero Chiang Chi Huei'. This came several weeks after Davis's last mission, but was the first indication of his fate. It also opened up fresh speculation about the identity of the MiG pilots, and suggested that some of the air regiments were Chinese. But nationality was not an issue. What concerned the American pilots was that there were more MiGs in the sky now than ever before, and that they were aggressive.

CANADIAN-BUILT SABRES INTO ACTION

The new F-86E could not reach the combat pilots fast enough, and some of these jets were manufactured by Canadair, which designated them as F-86E-6s. Lt Col Ralph E Keyes of the 336th FIS regularly flew this model, and he remembers the time he used one to shoot down a MiG, and nearly collided with its pilot when he ejected;

'I was 4th FIW Maintenance and Supply Group CO. I flew all my missions with the 336th FIS, and at that time we were flying the Canadian-built F-86E model. On 4 October 1952, there was a fighter sweep along "MiG Alley". Shortly after we crossed the bomb line on climb-out, we were notified of some very heavy MiG activity. We continued to climb to 40,000 ft, and about 40 miles south of the river we encountered two MiG-15s heading north. Blue Lead tried to close on one of them at full power but couldn't catch him. As Blue 3, I saw a MiG in my "three o'clock" position, and seconds later my wingman radioed that I should watch him because he was turning into our formation.

'I turned slightly right, causing the enemy pilot to pass about 60 ft in front of me. I opened fire, hosing his fuselage. A split-second later there was a small explosion in his engine compartment, but no fire and very little smoke. I turned hard left and came behind him in his "four o'clock" position. Locking on, I fired a long burst and, as I closed on his "six o'clock", I saw his canopy fly off, followed by the seat. Both narrowly missed my canopy and hit the side of my aircraft. The MiG pilot had already separated from the seat and passed about ten feet under my right wing. He was clad in a bright flying suit, but no helmet. He had red hair, his arms were flailing and his cheeks were puffed out.

'As this ejection occurred at about Mach One and above 40,000 ft, this situation would normally have been fatal. As I passed over him, I looked back and noticed his 'chute deploying. I turned my F-86 around and came back for a gun camera picture. He appeared unconscious, with his head down on his chest and arms dangling by his side.

The temperature outside my cockpit was about -40°C. There was no sign of an oxygen mask on the pilot's face. I assumed he died from the cold and lack of oxygen.

'This was a confirmed MiG-15 kill. Ten years later I ran into Col James K Johnson, who had been 4th FIW CO at the time. He told me that my description of the pilot and his flight gear was confirmed to be that of a Russian "honcho" flying from a base in Manchuria. There were only two kills that day, and the other was scored by future top ace, Capt Pete Fernandez.'

During the summer of 1952, the fighter-bomber activity was proceeding at full pace. There were plenty of F-84s in-theatre, and the 8th FBW had a large fleet of F-80Cs. In addition, the 18th FBW had all the F-51 Mustangs available, except for those operated by the Republic of Korea Air Force. This combination could deliver a lot of destruction in a day. The B-29s had destroyed most strategic targets in North Korea by then, which freed up the night-flying Superfortresses to pound the river bridges and roads, and thus sap the Chinese capacity to mount an effective ground offensive. This left

BELOW *Maj Ted S Coberly, CO of the 334th FIS, poses beside his F-86 at Kimpo in the summer of 1952. During the early part of his tour, before he assumed command, Coberly was credited with two MiG-15s destroyed, hence the kill symbols painted on the fuselage of his jet. His second kill came on 13 December 1951 during the mission on which Maj George Davis scored his tenth victory to become the war's first double ace (Ted Coberly)*

RIGHT *Lt Martin J Bambrick (left) beside his F-86 after a long mission. He had already been credited with a kill on 4 September 1952, as shown by the symbol painted on the aircraft. By this time the 4th had phased out its A-models in favour of F-86Es (Martin Bambrick)*

the MiG-15 pilots with only one alternative – break through the F-86 screen and destroy the fighter-bombers.

On 13 May the 4th FIG experimented with the use of Sabres to deliver bombs in the close support role, but on the day's final mission, 4th FIG CO Col Walker H Mahurin was shot down by flak over the Kumu-ri railroad yards and became a PoW.

'LAST LIGHT RECONNAISSANCE'

Sabre pilot, Lt John Ridout looks back on that period, and recalls a particular type of mission that was unpopular with pilots;

'The MiGs rarely engaged us except to get to the fighter-bombers. With notable individual exceptions, the average skill level of these pilots was substantially inferior to ours. They were not using cohesive team tactics, and seemed significantly deficient in instrument flight skills. They seemed reluctant to enter cloud, even when under close attack by F-86s.

'While I was with the 334th FIS, one of the least popular duties was "last light reconnaissance" sweeps. This involved sending two or four aircraft to "MiG Alley" just

before dark to observe the MiG bases in Manchuria. From the information gathered, our intelligence types tried to estimate the level of enemy activity likely the next day. It was a very lonesome feeling to be 200 miles from home base, knowing you had a limited fuel supply, and that the enemy knew exactly what your remaining time over target was.

'Our normal routine was to withdraw when our fuel load was reduced to 1200 lbs. This was adequate for a safe return flight, a power-on landing approach and a modest reserve for contingencies. It didn't give much comfort to find yourself in this position with MiGs coming up to engage. The only intelligent tactic was to bug out for home! I recall one mission when I was flying wing on the flight commander along the south bank of the Yalu near the MiG base at Antung. You could easily see the parked aircraft on the ground from about 20,000 ft.

'There was a heavy cloud deck about 500 ft above us, which was just enough to keep the MiGs from dropping down on our tails, and from giving the anti-aircraft gunners too easy a target. I remember thinking that the setting sun reflecting off of the dark water, the clouds and

ABOVE *Maj Philip Van Sickle, 335th FIS CO, sits on the nose of his F-86 after a photo session for his pilots. Their recent scoring spree had enabled the 335th to draw ahead of the other two squadrons in the 4th (Karl Dittmer)*

AA shell bursts was one of the most beautiful sights that I'd ever seen.

'Suddenly, we were shocked to find four MiGs coming out of cloud right in our "six o'clock". Obviously, they had some good ground control intercept support, and these guys could handle the instrument flying just fine. The leader tried one burst, but fortunately the rate of fire of his cannon was slow. We flew through those flaming gold balls without taking any hits. Things soon got interesting, and we ended up in a very tight circle to the right, swapping altitude for airspeed. This was a basic Lufbery circle, with me slightly inside my leader's turn and the MiGs strung out behind us. This was a nice safe manoeuvre because nobody can get enough lead for a deflection shot until the decreasing altitude forces someone to roll out. Then it gets tough!

'This situation gave us a slight advantage, and my leader was beginning to achieve a firing position on the No 4 aircraft. At that point, No 4 reversed his turn. That made him a sitting duck for lead, but fortunately he did not follow him. We later decided the MiG leader had ordered that roll-out to bait us into giving him a clear shot at the possible expense of his No 4. Suddenly, I heard a loud bang right behind the cockpit, and I thought I'd taken a hit, but it was just the APU access door popping open. The G-meter was giving rather high readings, but that was a secondary consideration.

'The leader played that diving turn beautifully to get us transonic. At that speed and altitude we had better flight control than the MiGs. Low fuel made further engagement suicidal, so we headed south for Kimpo, where we landed without incident.

'When we were debriefed by intelligence, they were particularly interested in this change of tactics, and the fact that the MiGs were painted powder blue, rather than the usual unpainted polished aluminium. Several days later we were told that we'd run into a crack East German all-weather unit, which explained the radical change in form. They were reported by several other Sabre pilots from time to time, but didn't bring a significant increase in the general skill. However, it did reinforce the warning that some of their pilots were outstanding.'

INTER-UNIT RIVALRY

Following the conversion of the 51st FIW from the F-80 to the F-86 in November 1951, considerable rivalry grew between the two Sabre wings and, indeed, between individual squadrons. Such rivalries had also occurred during World War 2, when the 4th FG's Mustangs competed with the 56th FG's Thunderbolts. Both outfits claimed more than 1000 German aircraft destroyed (both in the air and on the ground), with the 4th coming out on top by the narrowest of margins. In Korea, the 4th

F-86F-30 JACKIE'S BOY was assigned to Lt Edwin J Scarff of the 334th FIS at Kimpo in late 1952. On the war's final day, Scarff was one of many Sabre pilots flying top cover for photo-reconnaissance missions intended to ensure that the enemy did not bring additional aircraft into North Korean bases before the cease-fire came into effect (Bruno Giordano)

RIGHT *What looks like a derelict hulk is actually Capt Maynard Stogdill's Sabre undergoing major maintenance out in the open. The demands placed on F-86 units were exceptional, especially in April 1952 when over 400 MiG-15s were based at Antung, in Manchuria. However, it was not until the final months of the war that the USAF possessed sufficient Sabres to allow the 8th and 18th FBWs to convert to the F-86F, thus doubling the air force's in-theatre strength to four wings equipped with the North American fighter (Jimmie Pierce)*

BELOW RIGHT *Fuelled and ready for another combat air patrol over north-west Korea, a well-used F-86F-1 rests on the 334th FIS flightline at K-14. US Government accounting offices determined that it cost nearly $12,000,000 to operate the 4th FIW in Korea between January and June 1953. The constant replacement of expended drop tanks alone accounted for approximately half this amount! (Robert Odle)*

was at it again, and the 'Battle of the Stats' involved all units, down to the individual flights within a squadron.

And amongst those flights, there was one exceptional outfit within the 335th FIS – 'D Flight', also known as the 'Mach Riders'. All the Sabre pilots were aggressive, but the members of this 'crew' were particularly so. Collectively, they had an 'attitude', which led them to devise their own emblem embodying a caricature of their unit CO, Maj Philip Van Sickle. The group included Capt Philip E Colman (four kills) and 1Lts Coy L Austin (two), James H Kasler (15th jet ace with six kills) and James F Low (17th jet ace with nine kills). Lt Albert Smiley (three kills) also flew with this elite group;

'I got my first MiG-15 when I was flying Coy Austin's wing. I spotted him and Austin didn't, so he told me to take it. That was our standard policy at the time. It seemed that I chased that MiG all over North Korea. Just about the time I had him lined up, he would pull up into an abrupt, fast vertical climb, stall out and then flip over on his back. I took several shots at him, and I'm not sure how many rounds hit him squarely. I think the pilot probably ejected out of frustration! Anyway, Austin verified that the pilot was in his 'chute, so I got the kill.'

'With my second, I was still flying wing. Phil Colman was leading the flight and Kasler was leading the element. It was a repeat scenario of my first kill. Kasler first spotted the MiGs over Antung. "Casey" Colman still hadn't spotted them, so he told Kasler to take them. I was flying Kasler's wing. In a matter of minutes he'd lined up on one of the MiGs, which was apparently getting ready for the landing pattern at Antung. As I saw him scoring hits on his target, this MiG came out of nowhere and slid in behind Kasler. He was lined up to fire when I called to Kasler to break. Either he didn't hear me or he ignored me. The only thing I could do was to fire a warning burst in the direction of the second MiG to get his attention. I wasn't looking through my sights when I pulled the trigger, but my rounds impacted all over the enemy fighter. He was lighting up pretty good from all the armour-piercing incendiaries that were hitting him.

'The next thing I knew, the MiG's canopy popped off. The seat came out and there was the pilot, kinda floating back toward me, sitting in his seat. He passed by my left wing. My rate of closure wasn't too fast, so I banked over to get a good look at him. Apparently, his helmet had come off in the ejection. He had long blond hair, with what we used to call a "white side walled" haircut, which meant that the hair was clipped down to bare skin about an inch or so above the ears. He had to be East German or Russian. I never saw a 'chute, and my altitude when I passed by him was less than 500 ft. Kasler got two confirmed kills on this mission, which made him the 15th jet ace of the war.'

MAIN PICTURE *The Indian head badge on the fuselage of this F-86F-10 (51-2945) indicates that it was flown by the 335th FIS. Of the three squadrons in the 4th, the 335th scored the most MiG kills. Today, the squadron flies the F-15E Strike Eagle (Don Thiel)*

INSET *These 4th FIG Sabres are sat manned and ready on the alert pad at Kimpo in April 1953, the aircraft being all hooked up for immediate start. Scrambles were few and far between, but when they came, fighters were off the ground and at altitude in just a matter of minutes. As it happened, there were never any MiG-15s to intercept, just unidentified friendly aircraft (Bert Beecroft)*

Combat-seasoned 335th FIS pilot Lt Martin Bambrick examines the large hole made by a 37 mm shell fired from an NR-37 cannon fitted in the nose of a MiG-15 in June 1952. It only took a round or two from this heavy calibre weapon to blow an F-86 out of the sky. Indeed, Maj Felix Asla, 336th FIS CO, was killed when a shell ripped a wing off of his Sabre on 1 August 1952 (Martin Bambrick)

ABOVE *In the summer of 1953 the large number of MiG-15s available to the enemy placed a heavy maintenance burden on the 4th FIG, because its Sabres had to be ready to fly combat air patrols day after day. There were many more pilots than aircraft to crew them, and they were anxious to fly the missions, complete their tour and go home. These men are servicing the aircraft's radio transmitter unit, having first removed the electronics bay access panel*
(Bert Beecroft)

ABOVE Photographed out on the 334th FIS flightline at Kimpo, Lt Marvin Lamb prepares for his next mission. Lamb survived this and other sorties in Korea, only to be killed in an F-100 accident post-war (Don Showen)

LEFT An element of F-86Fs return from a late afternoon patrol over North Korea with their external fuel tanks in place – the MiGs were not flying that day (Gobel James)

MAIN PICTURE *Lt Stillman V Taylor's Sabre "Miss Priss" displays the 335th FIS Indian head badge at Kimpo in May 1953. During this month F-86 pilots were credited with 58.5 aerial kills, which was their third-highest monthly score of the war. The following month's tally was to be the highest (Stillman V Taylor)*

INSET *A flight of four F-86As are seen on the alert pad at Kimpo in the early summer of 1952. The example in the foreground (49-1257) displays two kill markings, and survived the war to serve with the 121st FIS, Washington DC Air National Guard, in 1954 (William K Thomas)*

OPPOSITE *This group of 335th FIS pilots, seen at Kimpo in the spring of 1953, includes Lt Bert Beecroft (back row, middle) and Capt Dewey Durnford USMC (front row, middle). Durnford's leather flight jacket displays the emblem of Marine Corps fighter unit VMF-311, with whom he had flown F9F Panthers prior to his USAF exchange stint (Norman Green)*

LEFT *Another well-worded sign at Kimpo. This particular board hung above the entrance to the 4th FIG HQ building. Statistics reveal that the 4th was the outfit to beat in terms of aerial successes, thus making good its claim to be 'Fourth But First'! (Larry Hendel)*

BELOW LEFT *Capt Vince Stacy flew with the 335th FIS, and was credited with 1.5 confirmed MiG-15 kills, which he scored in early 1953. January to March represented a particularly busy time for the USAF fighter force in Korea, with F-86 pilots registering a total of 99.5 kills during this period (Robert D Carter)*

RIGHT *Col Harrison R Thyng (right) was the 4th FIW CO between November 1951 and early October 1952. He was highly respected both as a leader and as a fighter pilot, and his exploits in Spitfires over North Africa and the Mediterranean in World War 2 were legendary. During his stint with the 4th, Thyng shot down five MiG-15s to become an ace. The second individual in this photograph was the adjutant of No 77 Sqn (Gordon Beem)*

OPPOSITE *Lt Robert 'Doug' Carter, complete with Colt 0.45-cal government-issue automatic and nylon flight jacket, is pictured with his F-86 Sabre at Kimpo. He shared credit for two MiG kills while flying with the 335th FIS (Robert D Carter)*

BELOW RIGHT *A good view of the tail numbers of four 336th FIS Sabres on the Kimpo alert pad. The closest three aircraft are F-86F-30s, which was one of the last models of the Sabre to see combat over Korea. 51-2894, on the other hand, was an early model F-86F-1, which had probably seen a lot of action by this time (Richard Keener)*

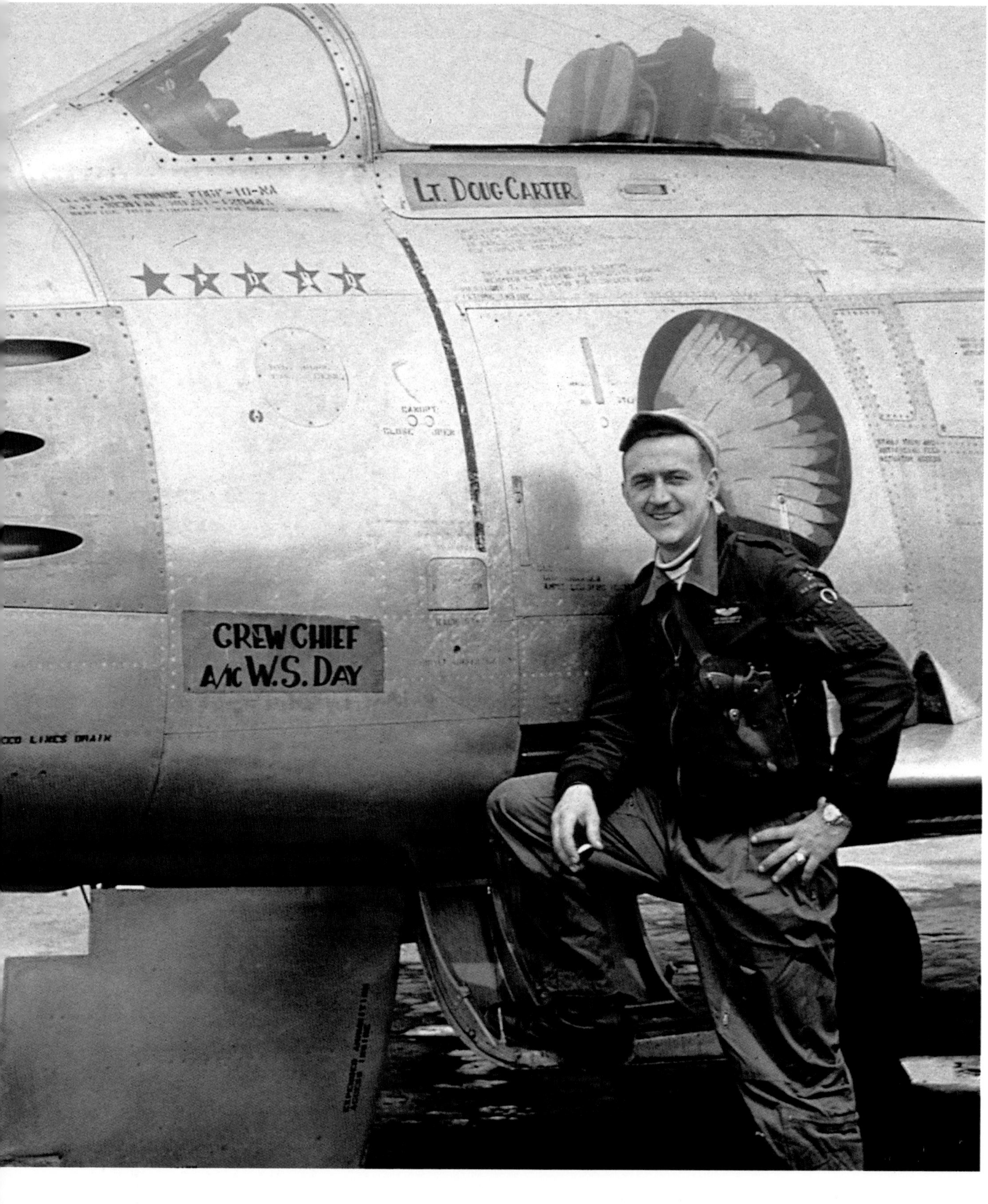
LT. DOUG CARTER
CREW CHIEF
A/1C W.S. DAY

This brand new F-86F-10 (51-12941) has just arrived at Tsuiki AB, Japan, from the US, and is being prepared for combat duty with the 4th FIW at Kimpo. It was later assigned to the wing CO, Col James K Johnson, who was a double Korean War ace with ten confirmed kills (Jeff Dibrell)

RIGHT *The son of American artist Norman Rockwell evidently inherited quite a bit of his father's prodigious talent judging by this mural, which was painted in the 4th FIW HQ building at Kimpo in the spring of 1953 (Richard Keener)*

BELOW *These two officers represent 335th FIS 'top management' – CO Maj Philip Van Sickle (left) and the squadron executive officer, Maj William K Thomas. Both of these experienced pilots scored a MiG-15 kill during their time with the squadron. The 'Mach Rider' emblem featured a caricature of Van Sickle. Designed by the squadron's high-scoring 'D Flight', it was only worn by the flight's 'select few' (Martin Bambrick)*

LEFT *Capt Cliff Jolley of the 335th FIS became the war's 18th jet ace, and he is seen here posing with his colourful hand-painted helmet. His F-86 displayed a 'Jolly Roger' pirate flag, as well as symbols for each of his seven MiG-15 kills (Karl Dittmer)*

Despite their aircraft being hooked up to external power units and their helmets ready on windscreen tops, pilots could never completely relax in the alert shack. When the order to scramble was given groundcrews and pilots got the F-86s airborne in minutes (Norman Green)

MAIN PICTURE *The Indian head emblem on this Sabre denotes that it belongs to the 335th FIS. This photograph was taken over the Seoul area a few weeks after the end of hostilities, and during a heavy period of rain* (John Tabor)

INSET Patty II *was an F-86F-30 assigned to the 'Rocketeers' of the 336th FIS at Kimpo. Standing beside it is Sgt James Lamson, a B-26 Invader squadron crew chief who was paying a visit to the base when this photograph was taken in 1953. Lamson painted quite a few outstanding pieces of nose art on 17th BW Invaders* (James Lamson)

Lt Don 'Dusty' Showen's SCREAMIN' EAGLE *is seen ready for the next day's mission in its revetment at Kimpo. The 334th FIS was re-equipped with F-86Fs in early spring 1953. These aircraft could reach the MiG's high cruising altitude, enabling the USAF to score kills that would have been impossible with the earlier A- and E-models (Don Showen)*

CHAPTER FOUR

AERIAL BATTLES INTENSIFY

During the final months of the war the USAF's score of MiGs increased significantly. There were several reasons for this, chiefly the greater number of MiG-15s in-theatre resulting from the enemy stepping up its training programme.

Both sides knew that the end of the war was months rather than years away, and because the conflict represented the best training ground for combat pilots, the pipeline was jammed. And, as recently-disclosed information shows, the Soviet presence had diminished somewhat since 1950-51. Therefore, by the early months of 1953 more Chinese pilots, and perhaps North Koreans too, were involved in the aerial fighting.

Statistics tell the story. Sabre pilots scored 99 kills in the first three months of 1953, yet the war's final quarter saw 170 MiGs destroyed. The fact that two fighter-bomber wings (8th and 18th FBWs) had converted to the F-86F during this time was not a factor because these units were still primarily involved in conducting interdiction and close air support missions.

THE EYES HAVE IT

On a clear day over North Korea it was usually the pilots with the keenest eyesight who had the advantage in combat. One of them was Lt Bruno A Giordano, a 334th FIS pilot during the war's final months. He flew with Col James K Johnson, the 4th FIW CO, and the war's 29th jet ace;

'I was blessed with exceptionally good eyesight, and this made me one of the guys Jabara and Johnson wanted as a wingman on the high altitude MiG sweeps. At this time some of the wing's Sabres were E-models, and the rest were the new F-models with the hard leading edge. Of course, the colonel was flying a new F, so I got to fly one too. It was my first time, and I couldn't get the engine started!

BELOW Lt Cecil Lefevers of the 336th FIS pulls alongside his wingman after gaining altitude following take-off from Kimpo during the war's final weeks. Note that the external tanks are in place for the long flight to 'MiG Alley'. Lefevers shared a MiG kill with Capt George Love on 30 June 1953. This jet F-86F-15 (51-12976) survived the war, and was eventually passed to the Nationalist Chinese Air Force on Formosa (now Taiwan) (Cecil Lefevers)

'The colonel had already taxied out and was ready for take-off when he radioed that he'd found a wingman, and that if I could get started I could be an airborne spare. The jet finally started, and as I rolled out for take-off a three-ship formation from the 336th FIS said they needed a No 4 man. The only problem was that they were flying the older E-models.

'As we got nearer to the MiGs we could hear a lot of radio chatter, and there was no doubt that a large number of them were up. We were in a perfect position to engage them because we got to altitude just about the time we were entering the combat area. We dropped our tanks, which left us with a full internal load and plenty of airspeed and altitude. My element leader spotted a single MiG which had just pulled up after making an attack on another F-86. He shouted that he was locked on, and we made the attack. I was flying his wing to keep his tail clear when, all of a sudden, the MiG broke hard and down to the left, spiralled and then did a split-s manoeuvre. Of course, we followed him down. Then he pulled out about 45 degrees, rolled over and split-S'd back the other way! We had never seen that done before. We pulled out right on the deck.

'The fight had started somewhere between 35,000 and 40,000 ft. But after the double split-S we were screaming along as fast as those birds would go. We were also as low as I cared to fly – all of this was over very rugged mountain terrain close to the Yalu River. We were chasing the MiG, and the No 3 man called out to me that he could not close. I told him that I was at 96 per cent power and he told me I could take him, so I moved ahead. I immediately pushed up to full power, and sure enough began to close on him. The No 3, who was flying my wing, called out that he was having both hydraulic and control problems. He had no choice but to leave, so I chose to keep going after the MiG.

'I fired a burst and it was so turbulent I got what looked like a shotgun spray as opposed to a concentrated impact with my 0.50-cals. It appeared that I only got hits on both of his wing-tips. A few seconds later, I fired another burst – same thing. I decided to stay with him as far as I could. I got down slightly below him and the chase was on. I guess we went from Suiho all the way down to the mouth of the Yalu. By this time he thought I was gone, but I was still below and out of his view. We were just about even with his base at Antung when he pulled up to the right. As soon as he did, it brought us above the turbulence. It was a tight turn with lots of G.

'I was about 1200 ft behind the jet when I fired a long burst right at him when he was square in the pipper –

ABOVE *Speedy Cec was named after its pilot, Lt Cecil Lefevers of the 336th FIS. At war's end, the 4th FIG had easily won top combat honours with the Sabre. It had logged over 30 months in Korea, eventually using all three fighter models deployed during the conflict. With the appearance of the E- and F-model Sabres, the MiGs were no longer safe at their extreme altitudes (Cecil Lefevers)*

335th FIS groundcrew remove the canopy from Maj Jack Mass's Sabre. Four of the kill symbols painted on the fuselage were credited to him. Some of the highest scoring F-86s were flown by several different pilots. This particular F-86F-10 served with the 51st FIW after the war, before being given to the Nationalist Chinese (Norman Green)

RIGHT With this 334th FIS Sabre's gun ports showing the evidence of a fight, the crew chief has written a temporary testimonial on what it has just achieved. This F-86 was assigned to Capt Leonard W Lilley, but on 14 January 1953 it was being flown by Capt Manuel J Fernandez, also of the 334th, when he scored his fourth kill. The latter pilot finished the war with 14.5 aerial victories, ranking him as the third-highest scorer (Larry Hendel)

BELOW RIGHT Lt Col Robert Dixon prepares to strap in for another Sabre sortie in the spring of 1953. At this time the 335th FIS was drawing ahead of the other F-86 squadrons in terms of kills claimed. By war's end, all three units within the 4th FIW had claimed a total of approximately 50 probables over and above the kills confirmed. It is believed that a high number of battle-damaged MiGs crashed while landing at their Manchurian bases, but this could not be confirmed (Norman Green)

and missed him completely! All the rounds went behind him. I made an adjustment and fired again. This time he was hit squarely. Pieces of his tail flew off and he snapped violently. Our airspeed was still over 500 knots. I pulled up and watched him flip over and hit the side of a mountain. In a second it was all over, and I headed back to Kimpo. I had no gun camera film, but fortunately one of the other pilots in my flight had seen the MiG hit the ground, and that confirmed the kill.'

The quality and aggressiveness of the opposition varied from week to week. Among the hundreds of MiG pilots who must have been stationed in Manchuria, there were a few who were every bit as good as their American counterparts. They were assumed to be experienced Soviet types who could not break away and fight whenever they wanted to because they were responsible for the less experienced pilots they were instructing. As it happened, the trainees had probably been enrolled in the most dangerous advanced training class in the history of air combat. During the final six months of the war there were more and more cases reported of MiG pilots ejecting as soon as an F-86 had locked on to their 'six o'clock', even though no shots had been fired.

Sabre pilot Lt Raymond Nyls of the 334th FIS had an opportunity to speak to a former opponent some years after the war;

'I remember those combat missions over North Korea, even though they were a long time ago. It appeared to us that the MiG pilots were undergoing some sort of combat readiness training at Antung. It seemed their aggressiveness would run in cycles of about six weeks. At first they were very timid, and would sit up there in the sun and study our formations, but make no effort to attack us. The next step was when they would become a little bolder, and an occasional flight would drop down for a quick pass on us. Then a little later they were very aggressive, and would mix it up quite well. All of a sudden the cycle would begin again, and it seemed to go on like that.

'I recall one mission when they were coming at us one flight at a time. One of our pilots got in behind their formation and shot down the leader of a two-ship element. Then the wingman bailed out without trying to evade! He must have been very scared, or his radio was out. But he made no effort to use his speed or manoeuvrability to his advantage. There were several similar incidents reported by our pilots.

'Long after my tour in Korea, I had the opportunity to talk with a former MiG-15 pilot who flew against the F-86s. He confirmed what we all suspected – that the MiG had a very nasty stall characteristic. They would go into a high-speed turn and pull it too tight, causing a stick reversal. They didn't have hydraulic controls, and it would do a sharp turn that would sometimes "class-26" (write off) the aircraft from the excessive strain. We noticed this manoeuvre and wondered how in the hell they could

ABOVE *Seen in the summer of 1953, the battered main terminal building at Kimpo provided a grim reminder of the events that had taken place at the base three years earlier. It served in this condition as the base operations building for the 4th FIW until war's end (Norman Green)*

keep doing that and get away from us. We sort of thought it was an aircraft control problem. In fact, we had much the same problem with the F-86A models, even with hydraulic controls, but we could control it with forward pressure on the stick.'

There were many 'top guns' to emerge from the six F-86 fighter squadrons in Korea. The three most prolific 'MiG killers' were Joe McConnell, Jim Jabara and 'Pete' Fernandez. Between them they were credited with destroying 45.5 enemy aircraft, all MiG-15s.

Fernandez had enlisted in the Army Air Corps in World War 2 straight from high school, but his first operational assignment was in the Panama Canal Zone after the war. He became an instructor at Nellis AFB, and it soon became obvious he was a natural at air-to-air gunnery. In fact, his uncanny touch was partly due to natural ability, but also to constant practice on the ranges near Nellis. His first encounter with a MiG was on 4 October 1952. In a matter of seconds he had positioned his Sabre for the shot, fired two quick bursts and destroyed the target. The second kill resulted from one long burst and the third from another two short ones. He often returned from a mission with ammunition left in his

guns. When Fernandez fired he usually hit what he aimed at. He became the 26th jet ace of the war. His father was Col Manuel J Fernandez Sr, Chief of Communications for the Thirteenth Air Force.

COVER FOR PHOTO-MISSIONS

Although the F-86 squadrons' scores were increasing, they could never ignore their primary responsibility of providing top cover for fighter-bomber operations. They also had to protect photo-reconnaissance aircraft like the Marine Corps F2H Banshees affiliated to the Kimpo photo unit. These aircraft always attracted plenty of enemy attention, probably because they were unarmed. Yet they were not easy kills – the Sabre cover, plus the experience and cunning of their pilots, saw to that. Lt Drury Callahan recalls one of these escort missions;

'My 37th mission was to escort a lone Marine F2H Banshee photo-recce bird. Engine start time was 1702 hrs, and we lifted off the runway eight minutes later. We climbed on a heading of 330 degrees towards the Banshee's first target, the railroad bridge at Sinanju. We crossed the bomb line at 1714 hrs and continued our climb to 30,000 ft, where we levelled off. As we approached the bridge, the Banshee began a let-down to 18,000 ft, which was his assigned altitude for taking the pictures. We followed him down, keeping him in sight all the way. Finishing his run, he swung left and headed up the main supply route along the coast towards Sinuiju, taking pictures as he flew. Halfway up the route our ground control radioed that a bandit track was coming our way, and to be alert.

'We didn't see anything, but Black Flight, which was ahead of the Banshee at 30,000 ft, reported that a formation of six MiG-15s had just passed below them, heading our way. There were large cumulus clouds and thunderstorms in the area, which restricted visibility, so Black Flight wasn't able to keep the MiGs in sight. It worked both ways – we didn't see them and they didn't see us. Nevertheless, we all dropped tanks and pushed our air speed up to 0.85 Mach.

'The recce bird decided to continue on his way. When he reached the Yalu, he turned right and flew north along the river, taking more pictures. We were almost at the Suiho Reservoir dam when it happened.

My flight, Baker Flight, was behind and slightly above Able Flight, which was providing close escort for the photo aircraft. We had them in sight, and as we neared the dam we spotted four MiG-15s coming across the river and making a pass at Able Flight and the photo-ship. The enemy had not seen us, so we told Able to break hard left. They did, and it prevented them from being shot at.

'The attacking MiGs then pulled off to the right and went above Able to set up another pass. Not seeing us, they pulled up right in front of us. They also broke into two elements, so we latched on to the high element. Baker Leader went after the No 2 man and my element leader went after the MiG leader. From this point on I can only relate what happened to my element.

'I stayed on Baker 3's wing as he came to his MiG from the rear. He opened fire at about 1500 ft and immediately got numerous hits. No 3 gave the MiG a second burst and got more hits on the tail and fuselage. At that point it began to smoke.

'While this was happening I was covering my leader, and looking around to make sure that nobody sneaked

BELOW Lt Bert Beecroft poses by the 335th FIS Operations sign at Kimpo shortly before the war's end, when Lt Col Vermont Garrison was CO. In July 1953 the MiGs were less active than in previous months, despite the large number based in Manchuria. With their lower levels of experience, MiG pilots considered venturing south of the Yalu to be a high-risk activity (Bert Beecroft)

up on us. Sure enough, I saw two MiGs at "six o'clock" closing on us, and I informed my leader. When they got closer they opened fire, so I called "break left!" This caused the attacking fighters to overshoot, and they weren't able to turn with us. After about 80 degrees of turn, we reversed and saw the MiGs disappear in the distance. Our break caused us to lose the MiG which Baker 3 had been hitting. The last time we saw him he was smoking heavily, and probably wasn't able to land.

'About a minute later Baker 3 spotted four more bogies heading for the Yalu. We gave pursuit but were unable to close the gap. They were at least a mile away and hadn't seen us. We followed them for five minutes before two of them broke off. The other two stayed high. As soon as the two MiGs turned and started letting down, we cut them off. Baker 3 was soon on their tails, about 3000 ft behind, but my Sabre was much slower than the leader's, so I was way out of position and too far behind. When you get into a fight, all flying is done at full throttle, so if you have a slower aircraft you're going to fall behind. This upset me because the leader had run out of ammunition. If I'd been in range I might have gotten one!

'The remaining two fighters took no evasive action and just flew straight for Antung. My airspeed during the chase was 0.97 Mach, which indicates how fast the fight was moving. We headed for Kimpo, low on fuel. Everyone

ABOVE RIGHT *Capt Cliff Jolley (left) and Col Harvey study the flight schedule board in the 335th FIS operations building before suiting up. Jolley would become the war's 18th jet ace with seven confirmed kills, all achieved between 4 May and 11 October 1952 – an average of more than one per month (Karl Dittmer)*

RIGHT *On 21 September 1953 a defecting North Korean pilot flew a MiG-15 into Kimpo. He arrived without warning, and was on the ground before anyone was aware of his presence. Security personnel immediately surrounded the aircraft and covered it up. This picture was taken from the alert pad immediately after the MiG pilot had stopped next to an F-86 and shut his engine down (Norman Green)*

LEFT *Capt Manuel J 'Pete' Fernandez poses for another pilot at Kimpo in the spring of 1953, by which time he was well on his way to becoming the war's third ranking 'MiG killer'. Fernandez finished his tour with 14.5 kills as the 26th USAF pilot to become a jet ace. Even at this late stage, another 13 men would achieve that distinction (Robert D Carter)*

This photograph was probably taken during a long routine patrol up the North Korean coast soon after the war had ended. Such flights were frequent until late 1954, when the 4th FIG was relieved in Korea by the 58th FIW, based at Osan AB (K-55). During this time there were many reports of MiGs attacking RB-45 Tornado reconnaissance aircraft that were taking photographs near the coast. This F-86F carries 336th FIS markings (Richard Erratt)

RIGHT In 1953 the 4th FIG participated in the top secret 'Gun-Val' project in which several F-86Fs were fitted with four 20 mm cannon in place of the standard armament of six 0.50-cal Colt-Browning machine guns. These Sabres flew on combat missions with standard F-86s to test the destructive capabilities of the cannon. Although kills were credited to 'Gun-Val' aircraft, the enemy was unaware of the test (Paul Peterson)

BELOW Armourers load the four 20 mm cannon in this 'Gun-Val' F-86F. Note that the bottom gun port has been sealed off, with the top two containing the cannon. This was the only visible external difference between a cannon-armed machine and a standard Sabre, and would not have been noticeable to opposing pilots during a dogfight (Paul Peterson)

arrived back safely. The tally for the day was one probable and two damaged. It turns out that my element leader's gunsight was inoperative, and he couldn't compute either range or lead. Mine worked fine, but I never got to use it. I would guess we held contact with the MiGs for at least ten minutes, which would be considered a pretty long fight!'

On 7 June 1953, a combination of different Sabre types flew their first major mission when F-86F fighter-bombers from the 8th and 18th FBWs attacked a power station at Suiho, in North Korea. This was an all-Sabre show, as 36 aircraft from 4th FIW flew top cover.

The following month Maj Steven L Bettinger of the 336th FIS became the war's 39th, and final, jet ace. But he was shot down just minutes after this achievement and became a PoW – he was later repatriated in Operation *Big Switch*. MiG activity tapered off considerably soon afterwards. Both sides knew the cease-fire was due to take affect any day, and the last big air battles were fought on 19 July, when ten MiG-15s were shot down, seven falling to the 4th FIG. The following day three more MiGs were destroyed, and this time the 4th claimed all of them. Finally, on 22 July three kills were credited to the 51st FIW. They were the last MiGs to fall in the Korean War. Five days later the war ended.

But there was to be no let-up on 27 July, especially for the fighter-bomber squadrons. The cease-fire terms were intended to prevent either side moving additional aircraft into Korea. But the communists were still expected to try to bring in as many MiG-15s as they could by last light on the last day. UN units therefore had the job of keeping all North Korean airfields completely inoperative, and F-86F fighter-bombers, F-84 Thunderjets and B-26 Invaders continually cratered any runways capable of accommodating enemy aircraft. The closer it got to sunset, the more intense this became. Most UN aircraft recovered to their bases after dark.

Appropriately, the two Sabre fighter wings had been busy providing cover for the operation right to the end. There was, however, one F-86 kill scored that day. At 1230 hrs Captain Ralph S Parr Jr of the 335th FIS shot down an Il-12 transport aircraft. It was the last confirmed kill of the 37-month war.

But the intense Sabre-MiG conflict still had a further twist in store. On 21 September 1953 a North Korean pilot flew a MiG-15 into Kimpo AB and landed before anyone even knew there was a jet in the vicinity. This resulted from Project *Moolah*, under which any defecting North Korean or Chinese pilot who handed over a MiG would receive $100,000, and be offered political asylum. The Soviet-built fighter was dismantled and shipped to Okinawa, where it was thoroughly tested. Eventually it was donated to the Air Force Museum at Wright-Patterson AFB, Ohio, where it resides today.

OPPOSITE *Lt Richard Keener is pictured outside the BOQ (Base Officers' Quarters) at Kimpo in 1953. He is wearing the standard blue nylon flight jacket which bears one of the most elaborate squadron badges seen in Korea. During the early part of the war the 335th FIS badge displayed just the round Indian head in the centre. From the late summer of 1952 onwards, the squadron opted for a much larger badge incorporating the arrowhead and arrow. There was little variation in the badges of the two other squadrons (Richard Keener)*

335th FIS pilot Lt Artie McDowell poses by his F-86F Loretta for a fellow pilot during alert duty. The right side of the aircraft usually displayed the name of the crew chief, with that of the assigned pilot on the left side – a tradition dating back to the early days of World War 2 (Artie McDowell)

Lt Harry Jones is seen sitting on alert duty in Maj Clyde Curtin's F-86F-30 Boomer. Note the five kill symbols painted under the windscreen, four of which were attributed to Curtin and the fifth to another pilot using this aircraft. Jones finished the war with 1.5 kills. Both pilots served with the 335th FIS (Harry Jones)

RIGHT *Many USAF fighter pilots shot down at least one enemy aircraft during the Korean War, and this list, posted in the squadron Ops building at war's end, shows the 335th FIS pilots that achieved just that. Although the 335th was the top-scoring unit, other squadrons also achieved impressive scores (Harry Jones)*

BELOW RIGHT *It was not all combat and R&R in Japan for fighter pilots based in Korea. These four 336th FIS pilots display their bag of pheasants shot just a few miles from base. There was no shortage of hunting 'guides' (David Price)*

OPPOSITE *An excellent view of a F-86 pilot Lt Rex White strapped in and ready for take off. The hand-painted helmet leaves no doubt about White's squadron. That this photo was posed during the summer is evident from the pilot's rolled-up sleeves. On a real mission he would be wearing his flight jacket to protect him from the extreme cold at 40,000 ft (Rex A White)*

MAIN PICTURE *Some of the sharpest shooters in the fighter business gather around 335th FIS CO Maj Philip Van Sickle, who is sitting on the Sabre's nose (Karl Dittmer)*

INSET *When the Korean war ended Lt Col Vermont Garrison was 335th FIS CO, and he is seen here (right) with his executive officer, Maj Foster L Smith. Garrison was an ace with eight kills, but Maj Smith missed this distinction by just half a kill (Richard Keener)*

The USAF's Korean War aces regularly made front page news back home. This news film is being shot after Capt Manuel 'Pete' Fernandez scored his tenth kill to become one the few double aces. These film sessions were staged, and not actually shot after the milestone mission (Jimmie Pierce)

Lt Bob Hartwig relaxes on the wing of his 335th FIS F-86F-15 before climbing into the cockpit. He has finished briefing the mission and is in full flight gear. Hartwig's aircraft is obviously a newly-arrived replacement because there has not been time to paint the squadron badge on it. This Sabre survived the conflict, and became one of many passed to the Nationalist Chinese soon after the Korean War had ended (Norman Green)

INSET *The mobile control unit was essential for the safe landing of scores of F-86s returning from missions – especially those with battle damage – and was always manned during take-offs and recoveries by experienced Sabre pilots. One of them, Lt Vernon 'Bud' Hesterman of the 335th FIS, is pictured during his time in the 'cage' as several flights of F-86s prepare to land at Kimpo (Bud Hesterman)*

MAIN PICTURE *Every 4th FIG pilot could be assigned alert duty at Kimpo, and they were always at the ready. It meant hours of boredom, heat in the summer and cold in the winter, but when the call came to scramble it was three minutes of sheer bedlam. This view of Lt Dick Keener's Sabre shows that all of the necessary flying gear was ready and within reach of the cockpit. The 335th FIS Indian head badge is also visible (Richard Keener)*

OPPOSITE *Capt Ralph S Parr, the war's 33rd jet ace with ten kills, shows Richard M Nixon the cockpit of a Sabre during the vice president's tour of Korea and the Far East. Parr was credited with the war's final kill at 1230 hrs on 27 July 1953, when he shot down an Il-12 (Donald Showen)*

LEFT *This 336th FIS Sabre (51-2747), pictured at Kimpo in early 1953, was one of the best-known F-86s to survive the war. It was originally assigned to Col Bud Mahurin, and carried the names Honest John and Stud on the port side. After the war, it was operated by the 35th FIG at Johnson AB. Mahurin was shot down on 13 May 1952 while flying another F-86 (Bill Boland)*

BELOW LEFT *The 4th FIW has always kept an Honour Roll of its top pilots and commanding officers, and this tradition is maintained today with its F-15E Strike Eagle operations. This 'Wall of Fame' was pictured at wing HQ at Kimpo during the war's final days (Norman Green)*

When Maj Jim Jabara completed his second successful tour in Korea, an up-to-date scoreboard listing all his successes (even probables and damaged claims) was painted on his F-86F-30 (52-4513). It was to be extensively photographed before his departure (Larry Hendel)

Appendices

NORTH AMERICAN F-86E SABRE

Powerplant

one General Electric J47-GE-13 axial-flow
turbojet rated at 5200-lb (2359-kg)

Performance

maximum speed 679 mph (1093 km/h) at
sea level, 601 mph (967 km/h) at 35,000 ft
(10,870 m); average cruise speed 537 mph
(864 km/h); initial climb 7250 ft feet per minute
(36.83 m per second); time to 30,000 ft
(9145 m) 6.3 minutes; service ceiling 47,200 ft
(14,385 m); combat radius (internal fuel)
321 miles (517 km), with drop tanks 424 miles
(682 km), ferry range 1022 miles (1645 km)

Weights

empty, 10,845 lb (4919 kg)
loaded (clean), 14,856 lb (6739 kg)
maximum loaded, 17,806 lb (8077 kg)

Dimensions

Span: 37 ft 1.5 in (11.31 m)
Wing Area: 287.9 sq ft (26.74 m^2)
Length: 37 ft 6.5 in (11.44 m)
Height: 14 ft 9.5 in (4.51 m)

Armament

six 0.50-in (12.7 mm) Colt-Browning M-3
machine guns, with 267 rounds of ammunition for
each gun; provision for two 1000-lb (453.6-kg)
bombs or sixteen 5-in (12.7 cm) rockets

SABRE STATISTICS

The 4th FIW's Kills

When the Korean War ended on 27 July 1953, a total of
39 F-86 pilots had been officially recognised as aces. An
elite group, these men had been credited with a
combined score of 305.5 kills. This represented an
average of over 7.5 kills per pilot. Listed below are the
scores of the 4th FG's three squadrons, as well as its two
HQ flights;

334th FIS – 142.5
335th FIS – 218.5
336th FIS – 120.5
4th FIG HQ – 20.5
4th FIW HQ – 4.0

Total – 506.0
(total UN Korean War air-to-air kills – 825.5)

4th FIW IN KOREA KEY DATES

1950

13 December 4th FIG CO Lt Col John Meyer leads advance detachment 'A' from Johnson AB, Japan, to Kimpo AB, South Korea, for the first orientation flight over enemy-held territory

17 December Lt Col Bruce Hinton, 336th FIS CO, becomes the first Sabre pilot to shoot down a MiG-15

22 December USAF loses its first F-86, but later in the day the first major air battle between jet fighters results in the destruction of six MiGs with no Sabres shot down

31 December after two weeks of combat the 4th FIG logs 234 sorties, engaging MiGs on 76 of them, and scoring eight victories and two probables for the loss of one Sabre

1951

6 March 334th FIS begins operations from Suwon AB (K-13), the move from Japan being completed on 10 March

12 April F-86s (and F-84s) escort 39 B-29s in attack on railway bridge, shooting down four MiG-15s – B-29 gunners 'bag' six

22 April 36 MiGs jump 12 low-on-fuel Sabres, but four are shot down and no F-86s lost

1 May 334th FIS returns to Johnson AB after being relieved at Suwon by the 335th FIS

20 May Capt James Jabara shoots down two MiG-15s to become the first jet ace, despite one drop tank failing to disengage

31 May 4th FIG Sabres fly 3350 sorties in first five months of 1951, and score 22 confirmed aerial kills for no loss

17 June North Korean Po-2 'bed check Charlie' makes night bombing attack on 335th FIS to inflict more damage on Sabres than MiGs have to date

9 September 70 MiGs jump 22 Sabres, and during ensueing combat Capts Richard Becker and Ralph Gibson become war's second and third aces

16 October 4th FIW posts its highest daily score so far with nine MiGs shot down

4 November during exchange duty with 336th FIS, Capt William Guss becomes first US Marine Corps pilot to destroy a MiG

13 November 50 Sabres meet 100 MiG-15s in two separate engagements and destroy 12, claim one as a probable and damage several more

30 November 31 Sabres destroy eight Tu-2 bombers plus three escorting La-9s and a MiG-15

13 December Maj George Davis of 334th FIS becomes the war's first double ace

17 December USAF announces that since the first Sabre kill, its F-86s have shot down 130 MiG-15s, with 20 probables and 144 damaged, for the loss of 14 Sabres in combat

1952

10 February Maj Davis lost while attempting his third kill of the day

31 March 39 MiG-15s shot down during the month at a cost of three F-86s

30 April monthly total of confirmed kills rise to 44, with four F-86s lost in combat

13 May 4th FIG experiments with the use of bomb-carrying F-86s in close support role, but loses its CO

July the last F-86A leaves the 4th FIG inventory to be replaced by the F-86E

1953

10 May Capt Manuel Fernandez of 334th FIS becomes the 4th FIG's second most successful pilot with 14.5 kills

16 May 4th FIG pilots shoot down 11 MiG-15s and damage six without loss to themselves

July 4th FIG F-86E-1 50-0625 becomes the oldest surviving Sabre in Korea, having accounted for 20 MiG-15s

15 July Maj James Jabara achieves his last victory to become the second ranking ace with 15 confirmed kills following his second tour with the 4th FIG

27 July Capt Ralph Parr of the 335th FIS scores final kill of the war hours before the cease-fire takes effect

North American F-86E Sabre

1 Radome
2 Radar antenna
3 Engine air intake
4 Gun camera
5 Nosewheel leg doors
6 Nose undercarriage leg strut
7 Nosewheel
8 Torque scissor links
9 Steering control valve
10 Nose undercarriage pivot fixing
11 Sight amplifier
12 Radio and electronics equipment bay
13 Electronics bay access panel
14 Battery
15 Gun muzzle blast troughs
16 Oxygen bottles
17 Nosewheel bay door
18 Oxygen servicing point
19 Canopy switches
20 Machine gun barrel mountings
21 Hydraulic system test connections
22 Radio transmitter
23 Cockpit armoured bulkhead
24 Windscreen panels
25 A-1CM radar gunsight
26 Instrument panel shroud
27 Instrument panel
28 Control column
29 Kick-in boarding step
30 Used cartridge case collector box
31 Ammunition boxes (267 rounds per gun)
32 Ammunition feed chutes

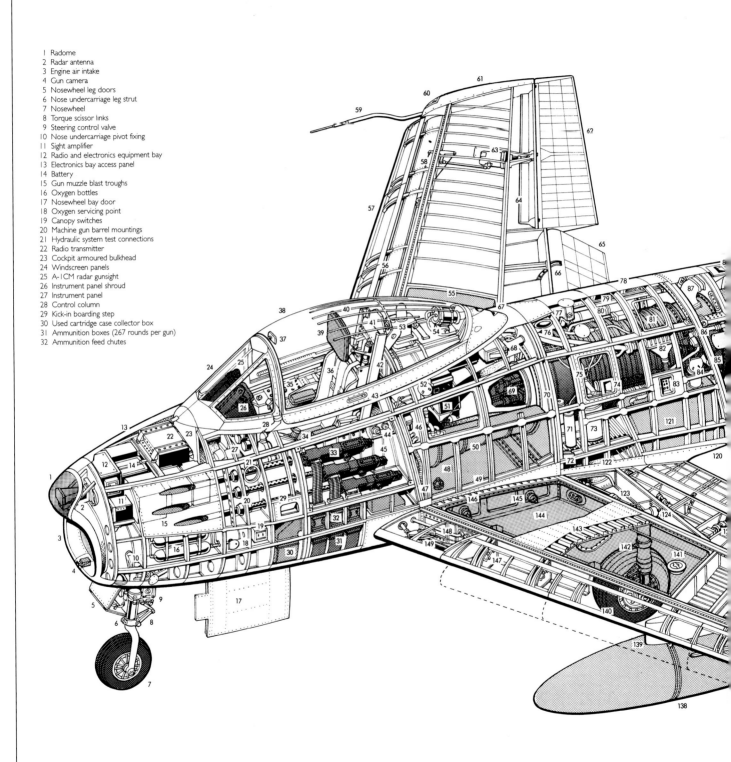

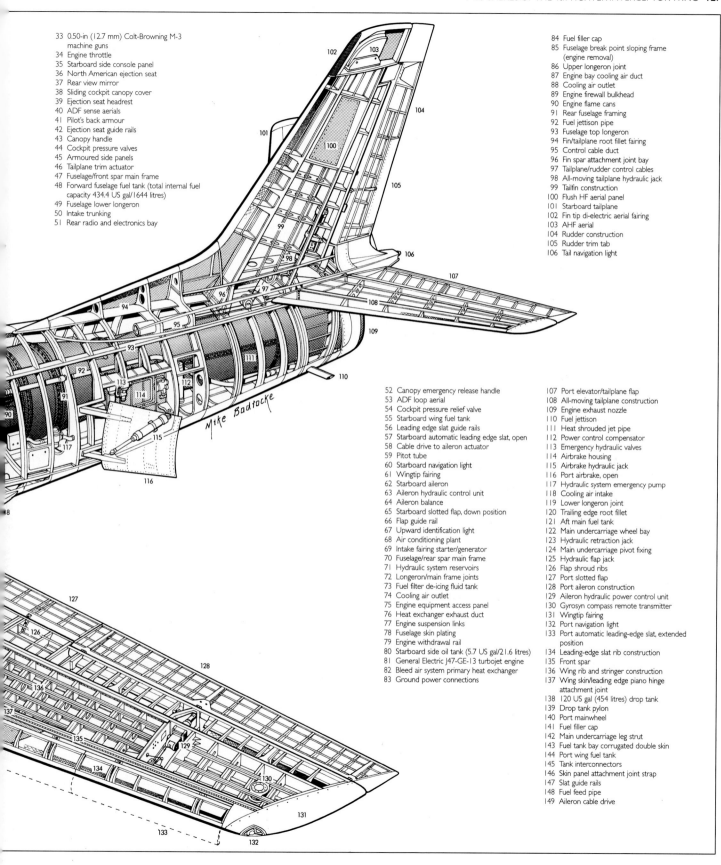

33 0.50-in (12.7 mm) Colt-Browning M-3 machine guns
34 Engine throttle
35 Starboard side console panel
36 North American ejection seat
37 Rear view mirror
38 Sliding cockpit canopy cover
39 Ejection seat headrest
40 ADF sense aerials
41 Pilot's back armour
42 Ejection seat guide rails
43 Canopy handle
44 Cockpit pressure valves
45 Armoured side panels
46 Tailplane trim actuator
47 Fuselage/front spar main frame
48 Forward fuselage fuel tank (total internal fuel capacity 434.4 US gal/1644 litres)
49 Fuselage lower longeron
50 Intake trunking
51 Rear radio and electronics bay

52 Canopy emergency release handle
53 ADF loop aerial
54 Cockpit pressure relief valve
55 Starboard wing fuel tank
56 Leading edge slat guide rails
57 Starboard automatic leading edge slat, open
58 Cable drive to aileron actuator
59 Pitot tube
60 Starboard navigation light
61 Wingtip fairing
62 Starboard aileron
63 Aileron hydraulic control unit
64 Aileron balance
65 Starboard slotted flap, down position
66 Flap guide rail
67 Upward identification light
68 Air conditioning plant
69 Intake fairing starter/generator
70 Fuselage/rear spar main frame
71 Hydraulic system reservoirs
72 Longeron/main frame joints
73 Fuel filter de-icing fluid tank
74 Cooling air outlet
75 Engine equipment access panel
76 Heat exchanger exhaust duct
77 Engine suspension links
78 Fuselage skin plating
79 Engine withdrawal rail
80 Starboard side oil tank (5.7 US gal/21.6 litres)
81 General Electric J47-GE-13 turbojet engine
82 Bleed air system primary heat exchanger
83 Ground power connections

84 Fuel filler cap
85 Fuselage break point sloping frame (engine removal)
86 Upper longeron joint
87 Engine bay cooling air duct
88 Cooling air outlet
89 Engine firewall bulkhead
90 Engine flame cans
91 Rear fuselage framing
92 Fuel jettison pipe
93 Fuselage top longeron
94 Fin/tailplane root fillet fairing
95 Control cable duct
96 Fin spar attachment joint bay
97 Tailplane/rudder control cables
98 All-moving tailplane hydraulic jack
99 Tailfin construction
100 Flush HF aerial panel
101 Starboard tailplane
102 Fin tip di-electric aerial fairing
103 AHF aerial
104 Rudder construction
105 Rudder trim tab
106 Tail navigation light

107 Port elevator/tailplane flap
108 All-moving tailplane construction
109 Engine exhaust nozzle
110 Fuel jettison
111 Heat shrouded jet pipe
112 Power control compensator
113 Emergency hydraulic valves
114 Airbrake housing
115 Airbrake hydraulic jack
116 Port airbrake, open
117 Hydraulic system emergency pump
118 Cooling air intake
119 Lower longeron joint
120 Trailing edge root fillet
121 Aft main fuel tank
122 Main undercarriage wheel bay
123 Hydraulic retraction jack
124 Main undercarriage pivot fixing
125 Hydraulic flap jack
126 Flap shroud ribs
127 Port slotted flap
128 Port aileron construction
129 Aileron hydraulic power control unit
130 Gyrosyn compass remote transmitter
131 Wingtip fairing
132 Port navigation light
133 Port automatic leading-edge slat, extended position
134 Leading-edge slat rib construction
135 Front spar
136 Wing rib and stringer construction
137 Wing skin/leading edge piano hinge attachment joint
138 120 US gal (454 litres) drop tank
139 Drop tank pylon
140 Port mainwheel
141 Fuel filler cap
142 Main undercarriage leg strut
143 Fuel tank bay corrugated double skin
144 Port wing fuel tank
145 Tank interconnectors
146 Skin panel attachment joint strap
147 Slat guide rails
148 Fuel feed pipe
149 Aileron cable drive

Mike Badrocke

4th FIGHTER WING ACES

Pilot	Unit	Date of Fifth Kill	Total Aerial Kills
Capt James Jabara	334th FIS	20 May 1951	15
Lt Richard S Becker	334th FIS	9 September 1951	5
Lt. Ralph D Gibson	335th FIS	9 September 1951	5
Maj Richard D Creighton	336th FIS	27 November 1951	5
Maj George A Davis	334th FIS	30 November 1951	14
Maj Winton W Marshall	335th FIS	30 November 1951	6.5
Capt Robert J Love	335th FIS	21 April 1952	6
Capt Robert T Latshaw	335th FIS	3 May 1952	5
Lt James H Kasler	335th FIS	15 May 1952	6
Col Harrison Thyng	4th FIW (CO)	20 May 1952	5
Lt James F Low	335th FIS	15 June 1952	9
Capt Clifford D Jolley	335th FIS	8 August 1952	7
Maj Frederick C Blesse	334th FIS	4 September 1952	10
Capt Robinson Risner	336th FIS	21 September 1952	8
Col Royal N Baker	335th/336th FIS	17 November 1952	13
Capt Leonard W Lilley	334th FIS	18 November 1952	7
Capt Manuel J Fernandez	334th FIS	18 February 1953	14.5
Col James K Johnson	335th FIS	28 March 1953	10
Lt Col George L Jones	335th FIS	29 March 1953	6.5
Maj Vermont Garrison	335th FIS	5 June 1953	10
Capt R Moore	335th FIS	18 June 1953	10
Capt Ralph S Parr	335th FIS	18 June 1953	10
Capt Clyde R Curtin	335th FIS	19 July 1953	5
Maj Stephen L Bettinger	336th FIS	20 July 1953	5
Lt Charles G Cleveland	334th FIS	11 April 2000	5*

* Lt Cleveland was upgraded to ace status on 11 April 2000 to become the USAF's 40th jet ace of the Korean War following a recent review of a 'probable' claim submitted by him